YOU
ARE THE
F*CKING
SH★★★★★T

HEAL YOUR ANXIETY
ANGER & DEPRESSION
FROM THE GROUND UP!

MICHAEL HSU

HEAL
FROM THE GROUND UP

Publisher's Cataloging-in-Publication Data
provided by Five Rainbows Cataloging Services

Names: Hsu, Michael, author.
Title: You are the fucking shit : heal your anxiety, anger and depression
    from the ground up! / Michael Hsu.
Description: Rowland Heights, CA : Heal from the Ground Up, 2019.
Identifiers: LCCN 2018912169 | ISBN 978-1-949593-02-0 (paperback) |
    ISBN 978-1-949593-05-1 (hardcover) | ISBN 978-1-949593-03-7 (ebook) |
    ISBN 978-1-949593-04-4 (audiobook)
Subjects: LCSH: Self-help techniques. | Self-actualization (Psychology) |
    Success. | Life skills. | Emotions. | Happiness. | BISAC: SELF-HELP
    / Personal Growth / Happiness. | SELF-HELP / Personal Growth /
    Success. | SELF-HELP / Emotions.
Classification: LCC BJ1589 .H78 2019 (print) | LCC BJ1589 (ebook) | DDC
    158.1--dc23.

First edition, 10 9 8 7 6 5 4 3 2 1

❖ DEDICATION

I dedicate this book to all of humanity as it speaks to the core of our human experiences. My hope is for humanity to transform as we heal the world from within.

TABLE OF CONTENTS

INTRODUCTION

That's right. You heard me. You are the fucking shit. (Or if you are a child reading this then, "YOU ARE DA BOMB!") You are created by the infinite power of love. Your true self is your greatest gift to yourself, to your loved ones and to all of humanity.

If this is true, then why do you feel so crappy? Why do you experience depression, anger, and anxiety? Why do you feel like you are getting nowhere despite trying to fix your problems and emotions? Reading the following statement will begin to shed light on the answers to these questions:

Problems bring up feelings in us that existed before the problem ever happened

Our feelings often say something negative about us, but it is important to remember they are never true. The **F.I.S.T. process** described in this book will teach you the following:

1. How to FEEL and to IDENTIFY your feelings. by sifting out the "fluff" of your overthinking and help you identify your core feelings. Remember, these feelings you will uncover are never true, but you are just pulling out the weeds (your negative feelings and beliefs) so they don't overtake your yard (your true self) and control how you feel and think.

2. Identifying these feelings will enable you to SEPARATE from them, because they do not belong to you.

3. After you separate from what is not yours, you can then honor the power of your TRUE SELF.

Let us now return to the initial statement, "Problems bring up feelings in us that existed before the problem ever happened."I will use my own experience as an example to help you understand what it means:

My fiancée has a poor concept of time and is often late, which angers me because it makes me feel that I do not exist. The feeling of not existing, however, was there before I even met my fiancée.

After I have identified my core feeling, I regularly take time to remind myself that it is not true and that it does not belong to me. Another example:

Loud cries, screams, hyperventilating, and a series of nervous knocks at the door. As an innocent ten year old, these were the sounds that filled my childhood. Although she struggled with a severe panic disorder, my mother's anxiety became my own. As I fast forward to nearly three decades later, the revelation that I was indeed just a sponge finally shed light on my entire life. In fact, upon noticing that I wasn't quite myself one morning, my fiancée paused to ask me what was wrong. I explained and she told me to not intellectualize it, but instead, to feel it. In that moment, I felt mentally paralyzed, not even knowing how I would go about feeling. She responded by telling me to make a sound out of this feeling. When I did, I started hyperventilating. Right then and there, I knew the pain I was carrying all my life was the pain of my mom's panic. Her panic was about the fear of not existing because if she died, she would not exist.

My mother had absorbed the feeling of not existing from her mother. My grandmother, Fei Hong, was outcasted by her father in the worst way possible. After her father came back from military school with more status, he divorced and remarried someone prettier and more educated. Fei Hong's stepmother did not want her new husband to associate with his daughter at all, leaving Fei Hong to be abandoned by the familiarity she'd known and raised by her grandparents instead.

It was WWII and when the Japanese invaded China, Fei Hong's grandfather evacuated her to safety, taking her to her father's new home with her stepmother. Her father's first reaction to seeing his daughter was utter disappointment, knowing the reaction his second wife would have. With her life on the line, she did not matter. She is 92 years old now and for all the time that I have known her, she often sits with her body facing outwardly from the dinner table, subconsciously believing that she is not a part of the family. My mother, in turn, absorbed all these feelings and unknowingly made them her own.

What my mother experienced is a struggle that we all deal with from time to time: because she could not fix what did not belong to her, she inevitably felt like a failure. I, in turn, could not fix the pain I picked up from her, leaving me feeling inadequate and consumed with feelings of being a failure.

It is the feeling of responsibility for others that turns us into an emotional sponge for their pain. When we surrender this responsibility for others, we finally become the greatest gift to others by shining the light of our true self onto the world.

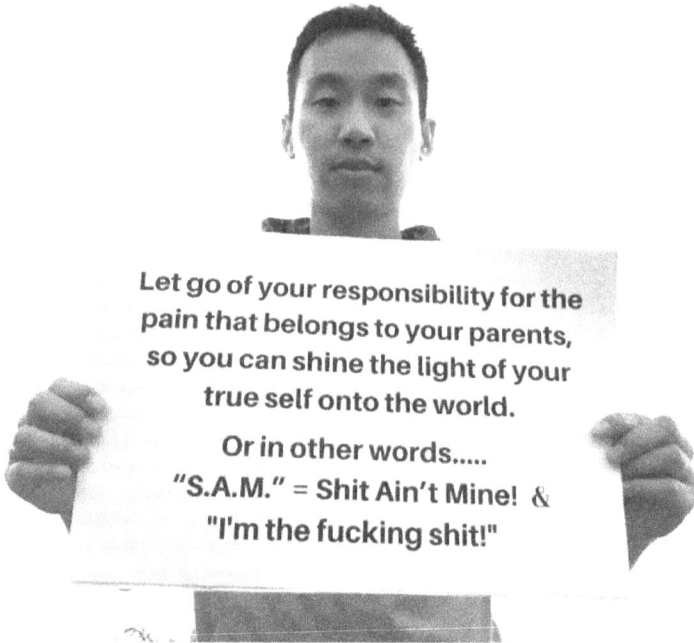

Let go of your responsibility for the pain that belongs to your parents, so you can shine the light of your true self onto the world.

Or in other words.....
"S.A.M." = Shit Ain't Mine! &
"I'm the fucking shit!"

WHY MY PARENTS ARE THE F*CKING SH*****T

What I share about my parents in this book is in no way pointing at what they did wrong, but rather, sheds light on the global phenomenon of humanity, where we all unknowingly take on and feel responsible for our parents' feelings. My parents have been nothing but unconditionally loving, supportive and caring to me all throughout my life. I love them dearly and forever appreciate all that they have done for me.

WORKBOOK EXERCISES

Now, I will introduce the emotional toolkit, F.I.S.T. (Feel - Identify - Separate - True Self),which will help you unlock your emotional strength. Applying it to your own problems and emotions as they arise,will help you get to the root. It will help you feel the peace you deserve. It is important that you take time to answer every exercise question in this book so that you fully immerse yourself in the F.I.S.T. process, reflect on "your" pain and uncover the truth as though you were in a private, face-to-face session with me.

PART ONE (F.I.S.T.)

FEEL &
IDENTIFY

*"Problems bring up feelings in us that existed
before the problem ever happened."*

"Feel and identify" is first about "feeling" as in the act of feeling. We are always consuming ourselves by living only in our head space with constant thinking, but we must balance our thoughts and actions with the act of feeling. After you commit to the act of feeling, you can then identify your feelings. These feelings will say something bad about you, but they are never true. All you are doing is pulling the weeds of your feelings so they don't overtake your yard and control how you feel and think.

To give you an example, my fiancée has no concept of time and waiting for her for when she is late often feels like a lifetime. This always makes me angry because I feel like I don't exist. This recurring and somewhat trivial problem brings up the feeling of not existing, but this feeling was there before I even knew her. My feeling of not existing, is not true, but the importance of identifying my core feelings, is so that they no longer control how you feel and think.

The first phase of F.I.S.T. is "Feel and Identify" where you will identify your core feelings by applying an emotional healing process, which I call P.E.W.F. You can think of the sound "POOF!" to help you remember it, as it helps you to truly separate yourself from these painful feelings like POOF! This process is important because it is a process that you can use at any moment of your life, as uncomfortable feelings, emotions and problems arise. Let us now begin in the next chapter and learn the first step of the P.E.W.F. process.

Note: If you are having conflicts in any one of your close relationships (i.e. your partner, your child) I highly recommend doing the P.E.W.F. process with the other person because it will not only help you understand yourself but each other. You will still perform the P.E.W.F. process individually, but you will be able to witness the true source of each other's feelings, which will change your relationship from a battlefield to that of harmony.

WARNING!

Before you begin with the process entailed in this book, I want you to know that the emotional healing process you will embark on in this book, may bring up feelings of resistance and doubt, but remember, resistance and doubt stem from over thinking, all of which help you distance yourself from feeling painful feelings. However, "pain" is not your enemy, but a wound that needs the medicine of love and guidance in order to heal. A wound, when avoided, will only spread and consume you with feelings of anxiety, anger and depression. Be patient and prudent with process detailed in this book, and you will uncover in a step-by-step process, the freedom, power and beauty of your true self and reason for existence.

CHAPTER 1 (P.E.W.F.)

❖

IDENTIFY THE PROBLEM

List one major problem that brings up the strongest emotion in you (i.e. anger, anxiety, depression or what I call "emotional suppression"):

_____

_____

Note: We tend to overthink our problems so describe the problem in one concise sentence. It also helps to think of a problem that brings up the strongest emotion in you.

Example: A major and ongoing problem I am facing is dealing with the fact that my fiancée can be selfish with her constant late behavior.

CHAPTER 2 (P.E.W.F.)

❖

IDENTIFY THE EMOTION

WHAT EMOTION DOES THIS PROBLEM BRING UP?

Once you have identified the problem, your next step is to identify the emotion that this problem brings up. I want you to reframe how you view emotions as:

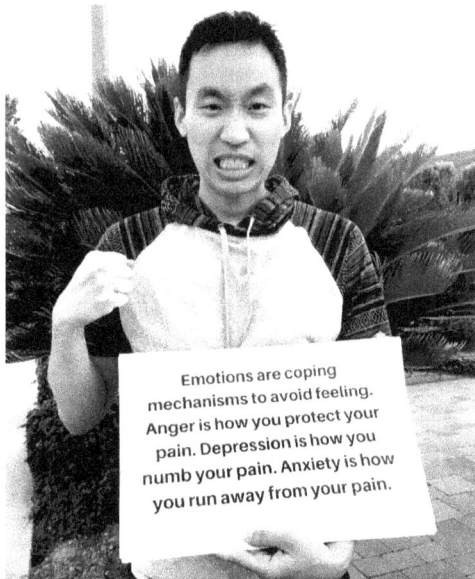

Emotions are coping mechanisms to avoid feeling. Anger is how you protect your pain. Depression is how you numb your pain. Anxiety is how you run away from your pain.

My fiancée being late triggers feelings of anger, because the anger serves to protect myself from feeling the pain of not existing and even projecting it onto her. The purpose of identifying your emotions is so that you can feel them and in turn, cultivate the awareness that you using them as a coping mechanism to avoid an underlying feeling.

When identifying your emotions, please choose from the following three main emotions, (anger, anxiety and depression), because they are the primary emotional coping mechanisms we use to avoid feeling the pain of our core feelings. Identifying your emotions, out of these three, will thus help you get closer in identifying the feeling that is controlling you. (note: Depression has a very strong stigma, but I define it as emotional suppression/numbing or bottling one's emotions).

You can also often find yourself identifying with emotions related to these three primary emotional coping mechanisms, such as identifying with the feeling of "frustration", which at its core, is really anger. Below are some more examples of how to identify your true core emotion:

1. Frustration, Annoyance, Aggression, Disgust → Anger

2. Fear, Worry, Nervous → Anxiety

3. Emotionally suppressed, numb / Sadness / Bottling one's emotions → Depression

List the emotion(s) the problem you stated earlier brings up in you: _____
_____

Example: When my fiancée *is late, it makes me feel "angry."*

(Note: Do not skip a step and list your feeling by saying, for example, "I feel neglected." Instead, choose out of the three emotions listed above, as they are the most common coping mechanisms to avoid feeling.)

CHAPTER 3 (P.E.W.F.)

❖

WORST FEAR

In order to uncover this underlying feeling buried within your emotions, you want to stretch your stated problem into your worst fear or absolute worst-case scenario. Can you visualize what would happen if everything you did not want to happen suddenly did, and in the most extreme way possible? What does this look like for you?

By visualizing this, you are getting closer to your core feelings, which, remember, as painful or real as they feel in the moment, don't reflect the truth. Think of yourself tending to your yard, knowing that by visualizing you are simply identifying core feelings and pulling out the weeds so they don't spread and take over your yard.

Before you engage in this yard clean-up, remember that it is critical to really stretch your stated problem into your absolute worst-case scenario. Regardless of whether you believe this worst-case scenario is impossible or unlikely, the purpose of describing your worst-case scenario is to address the core feelings that are controlling and consuming you.

Briefly describe your worst fear (i.e. worst-case scenario)

_____

_____

_____

My example:

Stated problem: My fiancée is always late.

Worst fear: All of my needs and desires are abandoned.

Examples of how to stretch your stated problems into your worst fear and absolute worst-case scenario:

Disclaimer:

The examples used in this book do not represent any one client I have worked with, yet are inspired by the clients I have seen in my practice and reflect recurring themes of our universal experience as human beings.

STATED PROBLEMS	WORST CASE SCENARIO
"I have been diagnosed with liver inflammation"	"Bedridden for the rest of my life. Death."
"I'm afraid I don't fit in with my coworkers"	"My coworkers hate me so much, they will work together to force me out of the company"
"My father doesn't speak English because he is very embarrassed of people discovering his accent"	"My father is on a stage and there are 10,000 people in the audience, all laughing and throwing tomatoes at him"

EXAMPLE #1:

A client once told me she doesn't know her true self since she is constantly morphing to please others. She stated her worst fear as simply that, never knowing her true self. This is not her worst fear as the reason why she morphs to please is because she fears being rejected or rendered unworthy. Her true worst-case scenario is everybody thinking negatively of her, leading her to believe that she does not matter or better yet, that she does not exist. More importantly, it also brings up more intense feelings of failure, because she feels she did something wrong to cause this.

EXAMPLE #2:

Another client described their worst-case scenario as "desperately looking for a job", which is an example of one's reaction to fix a worst-case scenario that is not truly a worst-case scenario. In fact, a more accurate depiction of a worst-case scenario to "desperately looking for a job" is forever being without a job. The reason why you can often find yourself desperately trying to fix your problems, is because you are ultimately wanting to avoid your core feelings. However uncomfortable it may be to envision your worst-scenario, its purpose is to identify this core feeling, so it no longer controls how you feel and think.

CHAPTER 4 (P.E.W.F.)

❖

FEELING ABOUT THE SELF

Now, imagine how you would feel about who you are, if, your worst fear (i.e. worst-case scenario), did, in fact, come true.

These feelings you are about to uncover are going to reveal something seemingly negative about you, but once again, it is not true, and by identifying it, you will no longer allow it to control you. As you are uncovering these feelings, remember, that you are just pulling the weeds out of your yard. In order to identify how your worst fear would make you feel about who you are, you should know that there are two dominant feelings that cause almost all of our pain (I will later explain in the book why these two feelings are so prominent, but first let's identify your core feelings.)

1. **"I don't exist,"** which means "I don't matter,"

    OR

2. **"I'm a failure,"** in other words: "I'm useless" / "I'm incompetent" / "Something is wrong with me."

If your worst fear or worst-case scenario came true, identify how it would make you feel about who you are by choosing one or both of the above feelings:

(Note: It is very common to experience both a feeling of failure and of not existing. For example, as I am writing this book, I constantly fear I will make a mistake and my book will fail, which in turn will prove that I am a failure. If I fail, I will no longer exist because, in my mind, my existence depends purely on what I produce.)

At this point, you might find yourself thinking, "What are you talking about? I don't feel like I don't exist or am a failure!" You may find it hard to identify your core feelings, while still fixating on a certain "problem" or the emotion of anxiety, anger and depression. However, if a problem is bringing up the emotions of anxiety, anger or depression in you, it only does so because you it is triggering a feeling within you that existed before the problem ever happened. Emotions, just as I mentioned previously, are coping mechanisms to help us avoid feeling the pain of our core feelings. Remember, these feelings are not true, so you do not need to resist it, but only identify it, so it no longer controls you how you feel and think.

FALSE CORE FEELINGS

You might identify "core" feelings as such, but the following list only reflects your feelings in relation to others:

> ➢ "I am unwanted...I feel neglected...I feel unappreciated...I am abandoned." (not how I feel about

myself; others make me feel this way)

➤ "I am insecure" (only speaks to my behavior and not the essence of who I am)

Note: Saying, "I am out of control" is not a feeling about who you are. Your worst-case scenario may be feeling as though you are out of control, with no agency over how things are done, leaving you feeling insignificant. In other words, you might feel like you don't matter if things don't go the way you want them to.

Now after you have identified your core feeling(s), ask yourself why you feel this way about yourself. This gives context to the nature of your feelings. Below are examples of how others identified their core feelings (i.e. their weeds), including the reasons why they feel this way.

Examples of Feelings that Do Describe Your Core Self:

Stated Problem	Worst-case Scenario	Feeling About Self
"I have been diagnosed with liver inflammation"	Bedridden for the rest of your life. Death	I'm useless, because it is impossible to be productive, being that my body can-not function

14

"I'm afraid I don't fit in with my coworkers"	Your coworkers hate you so much they work together to force you out of the company.	I don't exist and I'm a failure because I did something wrong to cause this
My father doesn't speak English because he is very embarrassed of people finding out he speaks English with an accent	He is on a stage and there are 10,000 people in the audience all laughing at him while throwing tomatoes at him.	"I'm a failure"
I worry my employees, whom I treat like family, are stealing from me.	My employees really do steal from me	I don't matter
Frequent marital arguments with husband	Divorce and son suffers tremendously because of it	I'm a failure because "I'm the worst mother in the world"
My father hates it when the people he manages at work goof off and don't listen to what he tells them to do.	He thinks he is always right. He doesn't even like it when his siblings talk about differing social, political or religious views that are remotely different than his own. religious views. His worst-case scenario would be to be proven wrong.	If he was wrong, he would feel "I am incompetent."

15

A young child does not like when her single mother invites her boyfriend over to their house.	She gets shipped off to boarding school in Siberia with no contact with her parents or friends.	"I'm not important"
Someone is making threats at my company	Someone harms my employees	I'm a failure because I failed to protect them

My example: Anytime I experience a challenge or a hurdle, I respond with a combination of anxiousness, frustration and hopelessness, while desperately worrying if I will fail to overcome it or not. My worst fear, for instance, would be to forever fail at everything in life, and interestingly, also, suffering from such poor health that my body would be rendered completely useless. For instance, when I do not sleep well, I panic, because it makes my body feel useless, a feeling that I already believe about myself. Also, not sleeping well makes me fear that I will die because it damages my health. The fear of death brings up feelings of "I don't exist" in me.

SUMMARY FOR P.E.W.F.

The P.E.W.F. process helps you begin to make those uncomfortable feelings, emotions and problems disappear like P.E.W.F. ! (POOF!)

a. Problem: State the problem that brings up the strongest emotion in you, for example, anger, anxiety or depression.

b. Emotion: Identify the emotion that this problem brings up. (choose from the following primary emotions that are commonly used to avoid feeling: anger, anxiety and depression)

c. Worst fear: Describe your absolute worst-case scenario.

d. Feeling about the Self: If your worst fear/worst-case scenario came true, how would it make you feel about who you are? Remember the feeling you will uncover is never true, but you must identify it so you know what is subconsciously controlling how you think and feel.

As I just noted earlier, I have this constant fear of failing and feeling of uselessness, as well as a fear of disappointing others as if I did something wrong to cause it. The question is, where did my feelings of uselessness come from?

CHAPTER 5

❖

APPLYING P.E.W.F. TO YOUR FAMILY

As you know from the story I first shared about my childhood, I first realized my feelings of not mattering upon discovering that I had internalized them from my mother's feelings of panic. In fact, years ago, my fiancée once told me something I never paused to consider: "You think you are most affected by your mother, but it is your father, who, in spite of how stoic he may be, unknowingly impacts you the most." Although I had no idea what she meant at the time, the reason why I was so unaware, was because my father carries tension and anger, which made it very difficult for to me consciously detect his underlying feelings. As evidenced by our relationship, where his presence alone made me anxious, his anger was functioning as an emotional TNT, preventing me from getting too close before it explodes. From my P.E.W.F. process, then, I uncovered feelings of failure, but where did those feelings of failure really stem from?

To provide you with a clearer context, my father is a person who is constantly working and even though he is already 71 years old, he identifies with being a workaholic. A year ago, he found out he had stage one kidney cancer and two months after his surgery removal of the tumor, he was back working full time. Throughout all the years that I lived at home with my parents, my father was deeply consumed with a mindset that could only live and breath work. He was so obsessed with work that he barely paused to say hello. This was never because he did not love me, but rather, because his focus was always centered on working and being productive, which was, in is his mind, the ultimate expression of love for one's family.

With the tendency to overreact when people did not abide by his "right" way of doing things, his anger would really bubble to the surface. Very similarly to my father, when I used to work at his pharmacy and his employees made simple, or what I thought at the time, were "bone-headed" mistakes, I too would get angry and furious at times. Moreover, my anger came from me projecting my own feelings of incompetence onto them, feelings which I had unknowingly internalized from my father.

Note: My father's emotional state has since changed dramatically for the better. He does not respond to life with the anger like in the past. Both of my parents and I have had invaluable yet extremely challenging family talks of how I have unknowingly internalized their pain. This truly shows the importance of discussing with your family (if they are open to it) how pain can be internalized in an intergenerational cycle. My father now sees clearly how I took on explosive angry reactions from him, and he knows how important it is to work on his own anger so he can set an example for me. I truly appreciate him for that.

"FAILURE" IS BEING UNABLE TO SAVE THE PAIN WE INTERNALIZED FROM OUR PARENTS

Since we are unable to fix the pain we internalized in our parents, we then project this responsibility for our parents' pain onto our children. For example, our parents feel responsible for us, in the sense that, if something bad were to happen to us, then they would be failures. We then carry this same codependent mindset into our children's lives, by feeling if something bad happens to them (death or failure), then we too, are failures. As you can see, this cycle bleeds through each successive generation, until someone realizes they are not an emotional sponge, but a beam of light, which I will touch upon in the following section.

With this generational cycle in mind, it is important to consider the role of both parents in one's life. For example, I only later became aware that my mom also fears failure, but in a different way. She is obsessed about the health and safety for her loved ones, because if they die, they don't exist, which means she has failed to save in others what she could not save in her parents. When I don't listen to her suggestive orders for my health and safety, for example, she gets angry. With both of my parents and their distinct fears of potentially failing, anger made it hard for me to consciously comprehend or empathize with the underlying pain they felt, only seeing the anger.

Ironically enough, a friend once suggested that I tend to treat my fiancée like a child and not a partner. As I reflected on his statement, I realized that I feel responsible for her, an attitude that is rooted in trying to save in her what I could not save in my parents. Like my mother, I too get angry at my fiancée when she disregards my advice and doesn't listen to what I tell her to do to protect her health.

Now, that I have shown you how I applied the P.E.W.F. process to my parents, I would like you to apply the P.E.W.F. process to each of your parents. Be patient with the process, and you will see its true purpose and benefit after you complete the process.

APPLYING P.E.W.F. TO YOUR PARENTS (EXERCISE):

Now, I want you to apply the P.E.W.F. process to identify the core feelings of your parents. Remember, you are identifying the core feelings of how your parents feel about who they are, not about how they feel about you.

The first step here is to identify the problems that bring up the strongest emotions in them (remember to choose between anxiety, anger and/or depression). The purpose of this exercise will make sense once you work through the following steps. (Note: if you have difficulty identifying a problem that brings up a strong emotion in your parents, it helps tremendously to work backwards, by first thinking of the strongest emotion you sense in them, and then, thinking of a situation that brings up that emotion in them the most. For example, if you sense anger in one of your parents, think of a situation that brings up the strongest feelings of anger in them, and you will have identified a problem that bothers them.)

Note: if you are having relationship troubles you will want to perform this part of the process together with your partner. It will give tremendous context to the source of both of your feelings which will allow you to better understand each other.

Apply the steps to one parent at a time, doing so in any order. Note: begin by identifying your parents' emotion(s) and then thinking of a problem that would most strongly bring up that emotion(s) in them.

(Even if your parent(s) are no longer alive, or have passed away when you were young, but still were the ones that raised you for a significant part of your life, I want you to still apply the P.E.W.F. process to them. Also, if there were caretakers who took the place of your parents raising you (i.e. grandparents) you can apply the P.E.W.F. process to them as well.)

Parents' stated problems:

Father:_____

Mother:_____

Parents' emotions (i.e. anger, anxiety, depression):

Father:_____

Mother:_____

Parents' worst fear (i.e. worst-case scenario):

Father:_____

Mother:_____

Parents' feelings about self:

Father:_____

Mother:_____

Note: it helps greatly to choose between the two most dominant feelings of either "I don't exist" and/or "I'm a failure." In addition, explain why would their worst-case scenario make them feel that way about them-selves. For example, if a parent's child "fails," the par-ent would feel like a failure themselves, because they failed in raising their child.

Your core feelings (remember, this is how you feel about who you are and not how others make you feel):

_____

_____

_____

Important: If you listed core feelings in your parents that you have yet to identify within yourself, ask your-self if you feel these feelings within yourself. For exam-ple, if you identified the feeling of not existing within yourself, and then, uncovered the feeling of failure as they pertain to your parents through the P.E.W.F pro-cess, pause and ask yourself whether you also expe-rience feelings of failure. Most of the time, it will be resounded "yes!"

Example: Jeremy stated problems at work where he feared he would be excluded and kicked out by his coworkers. The first core feeling he identified was not existing. Applying the P.E.W.F. process to his mother, whom he first described as calm, he noticed feelings of anxiety and anger when he remembered his mother taking an online test with just a few minutes to complete. The anxiety and anger reflected not being able to complete the test on time, which made her feel like a failure. I asked Jeremy if he ever felt feelings of failure and his eyes opened wide as he admitted to feeling this exact way all the time.

Michael's Parents' stated problems

Father: When other people make a mistake or don't follow his direction.

Mother: If people she loves don't listen to her advice about health, safety, and protecting against being taken advantage of.

Michael's Parents' emotions

Father: Anger / emotional suppression (possibly depression)

Mother: Anxiety/ anger caused by frustration

Parents' worst fear/worst-case scenario:

Father: Unable to work / my mother's death

Mother: Her death or death of her loved ones

Parents' feelings about self:

Father: Failure / don't exist

Mother: I don't exist / failure if her loved ones die

Michael's core feelings: *I'm a failure / I don't exist (My book will fail, which means I am a failure - If I can't sleep,* *my health will fail and if my health fails, I can't be productive. My body's inability to function when I have poor sleep feels like death to me; in essence, death is failure, because if I die, I can no longer provide value to others and become nonexistent.)*

PAIN ON TWO LEVELS

People may feel reluctant to apply the P.E.W.F. process to their parents because they can be fixated on the abuse and mistreatment their parents have caused them instead of identifying the problems and emotions they internalized from their parents. To which I tell them:

> *"There is pain on two levels. How a parent mistreats a child is one level of pain. The far deeper and greater level of pain is the pain a child subconsciously internalizes from their parents and thinks is their own."*

While the reality of the experience we know of as trauma is not as clear when we are immersed in it, (PTSD from war, sexual abuse, etc.) it manifests as a trauma once enough time has passed for us to acknowledge that it is wrong and traumatic. The trauma of internalizing your parents' pain and thinking it is yours is something you don't even know is happening. It causes you to enter a lifelong matrix of pain, because when you take on other people's emotional belongings as your own burden, it consumes your entire space and prevents you from knowing your true self. If you don't know your true self, you will feel worthless. In this matrix, you feel like a hopeless failure because you cannot fix the pain of others, especially if you think their "stuff" belongs to you. This, I believe, is one of the greatest traumas one could experience.

Remember, unhealed pain drives a parent to mistreat others and their children. A child is born with the gift of sensitivity, making them so intuitive and attuned to the feelings of others that they can feel all the unhealed pain underneath their parents' abuse, anger and depression. However, this is only experienced subconsciously and not consciously. As a result, they feel it so strongly that they believe this pain is theirs.

Interestingly, it is the unhealed pain of the abusive, angry, absent, or emotionally inexpressive parent where the child is most likely to absorb most of their pain from. A parent doesn't necessarily have to be abusive in order for feelings of worthlessness to be absorbed by the child. In fact, my parents never told me I was ugly, a failure, and that I did not matter. Instead, they pretty much smothered me with love. Nonetheless, I still felt all these feelings, because I internalized their feelings and made them mine when I was a child.

EXAMPLE #1:

What I am about to share with you, will be so tragic that it will be very hard to stomach. Still, I want you to use this story as a way to learn how the greatest pain is not exactly what happens to you, but is what you internalized from your parents.

Olga is a 40 year old woman who was sexually abused as a child by her very own father. Yet even as horrifically traumatizing as this was, Olga's greatest pain was still the pain she unknowingly internalized from her parents. She would often fear that an argument with her friends or coworkers would lead to them secretly disliking her. Her worst-case scenario was having a viral meme humiliating her to the point that it would lead to her banishment from society. If this came true, it would make her feel not only that she does not exist, but more strongly, that she is failure, because she did something wrong to be alienated. Moreover, her core pain of failure was internalized from her parents' feelings of failure, which I will detail later on.

Quite shockingly, when Olga finally opened up to her mother about her sexual abuse by her father, her mother not only failed to console her, but reacted by remaining in complete denial. Believe it or not, from the very next day on, her mother acted as if nothing ever did happen. This is not because her mother did not love her, but rather, because admitting to what happened, would be admitting that she failed as a parent. To begin with, she already worried about not only failing her daughter, but also her son. In fact, Olga's mother's worst fear was the death of her adopted brother, being that he is an alcoholic. If this were to happen, it would make her feel like a failure.

Olga's father's worst fear, similar to her mother, was her brother drinking and driving recklessly, dying in a car accident, which would make her father feel like a failure. Her father's feeling of failure comes from her paternal grandmother, who she considers "crazy." She is frantically worried about other people talking badly about her and is always thinking that other people are out to get her. Her grandmother's worst fear is to be outcasted by all, earning a bad reputation in society. Interestingly, this is the exact same core pain that Olga experiences in her everyday life. As you can see, your greatest pain is not really what happens to you, but rather, it is your parents' pain that you unknowingly make yours, when you were a child, that becomes your greatest trauma.

EXAMPLE #2:

Stephanie's parents have not had a relationship with her for 27 years, from the time she got married. Stephanie wants to overcome her longing for approval and acceptance from her parents. She feels unwanted because of the lack of relationship with her parents. She is worried to bring up sensitive issues with her own children, fearful of creating the same nonexistent relationship she has with her parents. If this were to happen, it would make her feel unwanted and more importantly, that she does not exist.

Growing up with her father, Stephanie remembered that if he did not have things his way, he would become angry. If he didn't get things his way, he felt as though he didn't matter. Stephanie's father's mother experiences a lot of anxiety when she doesn't get things her way. Stephanie was forced to live with her grandparents while she attending college, as the only condition related to pursuing her education. As you can see, it is not how Stephanie's parents mistreated her that has caused these feelings of not mattering, but really, the unhealed pain she internalized from her father. Ultimately, Stephanie's father's behavior only stems from internalizing his mother's pain and making it his.

GRANDPARENTS

Just as both Olga and Stephanie benefited from understanding their fathers by reflecting on the feelings of their paternal grandmothers, it helps to think about your parents' childhood and your grandparents who raised them. Apply P.E.W.F. to your grandparents. It will give context to how your parents' feelings were internalized from their own parents. In doing this exercise, you will realize that we are just emotional sponges to each of our parents' unhealed pain. Note: It is highly recommended to begin with identifying the strongest emotion you sense in them because you may naturally feel far removed from the problem. When considering these emotions, it helps to choose out of the following three: anger, anxiety and depression), and then think of a situation (i.e problem) that would bring up that emotion in the strongest way.

In the event that your grandparents are no longer alive however, it is still critical to walk through this process by relying on past memories and stories, insights from your own parents, and other information you can gather.

Grandparents' emotions: _____
_____

Grandparents' stated problems: _____
_____

Grandparents' worst fear / worst-case scenario: _____
_____

Grandparents' feelings about self: _____
_____

My father has always remained private about his side of the family. But when I finally explored the feelings of my grandmother on my father's side, I was able to learn a lot. My grandmother would look down upon my father because he "only" went to pharmacy school and not medical school. She favored his younger brother because she thought he was better looking and went to a better school. When my parents got married, the first thing she told my mom was that she will never be as pretty and smart as her other son's wife. Obviously, what she shared with my mom reflected what she felt about herself. More importantly, it is these feelings that my father internalized from her. I would like to reiterate that it is not how my grandma treated my father that caused him these feelings, but rather, that it is what my father subconsciously internalized from her.

CHILDREN ARE EMOTIONAL SPONGES

This section is especially important if you have children. Even if you do not have children, you will want to read this section in order to connect with your inner child and understand how your matrix of "other people's pain is my pain" originated. Moreover, because the P.E.W.F. process has to be explained to a child in very simple terms, reading this section will make the process that much easier for you to understand.

If you have children, you may be a parent who feels very troubled and purely focused on the well-being of your child, but feels incapable of fixing your reflection because you have yet to work through your unhealed pain. Feeling lost is a common sentiment shared amongst parents, but simply being aware of how your pain might be absorbed by your children means there is always a way to transform the dynamic of your relationship with them.

"Children are the symptom. Parents are the cause."

I very often have parents who bring their children to see me as clients, and it amazes me because time and time again, the child is carrying the same exact feelings as their parents. It's almost as if I get to see myself in the child and understand why I have suffered for so long with these feelings that weren't even mine.

If you have any unhealed pain, your child can feel it all subconsciously and will internalize it as if it is their own because:

"Children are the emotional sponge to their parents' unhealed childhood pain."

Parents must first work through their unhealed pain so their child no longer absorbs it. When parents have acknowledged and processed their feelings, their children are no longer absorbing them subconsciously.

Sadly, I have many parents who bring their children as clients, and the children have absorbed the painful feelings of their parents so immensely and for so long that they are virtually mute, or silent. The reason as to why they shut down so dramatically, however, is to prevent feeling the insurmountable pain of being responsible for their parents' pain. Doing the P.E.W.F. process with the family as a whole is life changing for all, but unfortunately, very few families have confronted or embraced the urgency for a discussion regarding this intergenerational cycle of pain, let alone, been aware that such a dynamic would ever pertain to their family.

APPLYING P.E.W.F. WITH YOUR CHILDREN

After you have worked through the P.E.W.F. process with yourself and your parents, you will be ready to guide your children through the P.E.W.F. process. Doing so will help them recognize how their feelings were internalized from yours. You may think your children are too young to do this, but the earlier a child knows about the pain they internalized from their parents, the better and more beneficial, because it is traumatic for a child to have to unknowingly bear responsibility for pain that does not belong to them. Remember, when you look at your child, you are looking at a window into your inner child and childhood, which will help reflect back to you where all your struggles began.

I once had a client who shared with me how he told his nine year old autistic son about his own unresolved feelings which he internalized from his parents. He let his son know that when he feels his father's feelings within himself, to remind himself it does not belong to him. His son responded by reaching out and holding his hand, saying "Dad, I love you. You are a good father." A parent telling their child, that the feelings they feel within themself, does not belong to them, is one of the most touching things you can ever experience. This validation is one of the greatest gifts you can ever give to your child and ends the intergenerational cycle of absorbing each other's pain.

GUIDING YOUR CHILDREN THROUGH THE P.E.W.F. PROCESS

Simpler Wording: You will need to guide them along the process by first using simpler words, so they can be able to understand. Here are some examples:

➤ Anxiety → Worry

➤ Worst-case scenario → Worst fear

➤ Depression → Push down your feelings (motion both of hands pushing down on feelings)

➤ Failure → "I can't do things right" or "Something is wrong with me"

➤ I don't exist → "I'm not important" or "I don't matter"

You will now observe me guiding a child through the P.E.W.F. process along with their parents:

IDENTIFY THE PROBLEM AND EMOTION

Yuri is a young child who doesn't like when her single mother spends time with her new boyfriend. The emotion this problem brings up in Yuri is anger. Her parents brought her to see me because they believed her feelings were caused by their recent divorce and separation.

IT'S JUST A GAME (I.E. WORST-CASE SCENARIO)

After identifying the problem and the emotion of anger that it brought up, I asked Yuri what her "worst fear" was (i.e. worst-case scenario). In preparing Yuri to identify her worst fear, I first told her we are just playing a game, and prefaced by reminding her that what I was going to say was not really going to happen. I suggested to her, that her worst fear would be to be shipped off to a boarding school in Siberia, forever, without any contact with her parents, while her mother's boyfriend ended up moving in and taking her place in the house. Yuri responded with her mouth opened gaping wide. The mother in turn smiled and then told her daughter that it's not going to happen. Remind your child that P.E.W.F. is just a game!

Pulling out the Weeds:

After you have identified your child's worst fear, ask them how it would it make them feel about who they are if their worst fear came true. Remember, it will normally be at least one of the following two feelings as they are the most common:

> ➤ **"I don't matter":** which means "I don't exist" or "I'm not important,"

> OR

> ➤ **"I'm a failure":** which means "I can't do things right" or "something is wrong with me."

You will want to guide them to this point if their initial answer is associated with any of these core feelings. Tell your child that the feeling they are going to uncover is going to say something negative, but that it is not true and that this game is meant to pull out the weeds from the ground. Even make the physical motion of pulling out the weeds as you are describing it, so they can better understand it.

Going back to my previous example, I asked Yuri how it would make her feel about who she is if her worst fear did come true, and she replied by saying, "I'm not important."

USE AN OBJECT TO REPRESENT THE FEELINGS THE CHILD HAS INTERNALIZED

After your child has identified their core feeling, use an object to represent the feeling they hold about who they are. Specifically, let them hold the object in their hands and tell that this particular object (i.e. this feeling) was there before the problem ever happened.

With Yuri, for instance, I used a handheld desk clock that I keep in my office to represent the feeling of "I'm not important." I pointed at the clock to which I called the "broken clock" and said it was there before her mom ever met her new boyfriend. Much like the clock, the feeling of not mattering only seemed like it was caused by the boyfriend's presence in her mother's life, when in reality, it was there before. I gently reminded the child that the feeling is not true, and that we are just pulling the weeds to clear up the yard.

SHARE YOUR P.E.W.F. WITH YOUR CHILD

After your child completes their P.E.W.F., it is critical that you tell them the details of your P.E.W.F. so they can see where their feelings came from, and eventually the P.E.W.F. of their grandparents. As a parent, if you identified feelings of failure about yourself, to name one, that were not initially uncovered in your child's P.E.W.F. process, then you will want to ask them whether they ever experience feelings of failure.

When I applied P.E.W.F. process to Yuri's mother, she described her problem by prefacing that because she is new to the hospital she is working at now, her co-workers will often skip over her and ask other employees that used to work at her position for help. The mother's reaction to this is anger because it makes her feel like she is incompetent, or more accurately, a failure.

I, in turn, asked the daughter whether she ever experiences feelings of failure, such as "I can't do things right" and she shared frustration about how she feels when she is in dance class and cannot get the moves right, becoming angry with herself. Here, you can see the daughter's feelings of failure and the anger she used to avoid feeling it, in how they stem from the mother.

Similarly, the mother notes that her daughter experiences a lot of anxiety and is constantly worrying about things. For example, her daughter does not like to wear short sleeved t-shirts because it exposes the freckles, although barely visible, on her arms. She is worried about what others will think of her if they see her skin even though they may never notice unless they were to get very close. For example, she feels self conscious when people look at her from the side, because she feels her nose is too big from that angle. (in reality, the size of her nose is normal and proportionate to her face (Note: the belief that "something is wrong with me," which is what Yuri admitted to in regards to her nose, is associated with failure, because if something is wrong with her, there is almost nothing she can do about it.)

After identifying the core feelings of the mother, I go through the P.E.W.F. process with the father and his stated problem is the thought of not succeeding at work or being a bad father. The emotion this thought brings up is anxiety. His worst fear is to be forever jobless and to lose his daughter because she might want nothing to do with him. If his worst fear were to come true, he would have no relationship with his daughter and would thus feel like a failure.

As you can see, the mother uses anger to avoid the feeling of failure and the father uses anxiety to avoid the same feeling of failure. Interestingly enough, the strong emotions of anger and anxiety that they experience come up in their daughter's life experiences and recur to avoid this feeling of failure.

In order to bring everything together, I revisited the original issue of Yuri being angry when her single mother spent time with her boyfriend. I asked Yuri if she felt as though she did something wrong to cause this, as if something is wrong with her and she responded "yes." As you can see, Yuri's feelings of "I'm not important" were rooted in the feeling of failure, as in "something is wrong with me." Above all, Yuri's feelings of failure were internalized by both of her parents and were in turn unknowingly absorbed by her.

Note: It is very eye-opening to – instead of telling your child your core feelings – first have him/her apply the P.E.W.F. process to you. Learning how your children see you helps you understand how intuitive and sensitive they are about how you feel. Also, it is important that your child learns how to apply the P.E.W.F. process because it helps them see how they are possibly misusing their gift of sensitivity as an emotional sponge for the pain of others.

ALL CHILDREN ARE BORN WITH THE GIFT OF SENSITIVITY

To communicate to Yuri how her feelings were internalized from her parents, I took the same desk clock, representative of her feeling of "I'm a failure" or "I'm not important," and proceeded to ask her, whose broken clock is this? Yuri replied by saying that it is her parents' broken clock. I then asked, how did this broken clock end up on her lap? The child put up what I refer to as her "emotional antennas," the gift of sensitivity every child is born with. These emotional antennas allow children to feel what others feel, namely their parents. However, if there is no one to tell them that they possess this gift, they feel everything their parents feel, as if it is theirs. I then asked her if she can fix this broken clock, and she said "no," because it is not hers. The purpose of this conversation was all to train Yuri to understand that her feelings do not belong to her, thereby undoing her greatest pain.

If you have children, answer their P.E.W.F. here:

Your child's stated problems: _____

_____

Your child's emotions: _____

_____

Your child's worst fear: _____

_____

Your child's feeling about self: _____

_____

Example #2: A 12 year old boy is having severe anger issues in school where he will blow up emotionally and take it out on others. The parents experience anger when they don't get things their way, because it makes them feel like they don't exist. The child here is just absorbing the parents' pain and making it his own, resulting in an outburst because the child also experiences anger when he doesn't get things his way. I want you to really feel this. The child is trying to fix their parents' anger and feelings of not existing by living it. It is a nightmare for the helpless child because there is nothing that child can do to fix what doesn't belong to him in the first place.

THE INTERGENERATIONAL CYCLE

Your core feelings: _____

_____

Your father's core feelings: _____

_____

Your mother's core feelings: _____

_____

Your grandparents' core feelings: _____

_____

Your children's core feelings (if you have children):

_____

_____

Do you see the pattern now? Each generation is harboring the same feelings because each generation is just subconsciously absorbing each of their parents' feelings and is unknowingly taking ownership of pain that never belonged to them.

EXAMPLES OF P.E.W.F.:

Below are a few examples of people going through the P.E.W.F. process, in order to facilitate you as you complete your process of P.E.W.F.

EXAMPLE #1:

Yoshi has been diagnosed with inflammation in his liver. It brings up the emotion of depression. His worst-case scenario would be being bedridden and unable to speak or move. If this came true, it would make him feel useless because he has no way of being productive with a body that cannot function.

Yoshi's mother doesn't like practicing her English in front of others because she is embarrassed and gets angry at herself if they were to catch her speaking with an accent. Her worst-case scenario would be speaking English on a stage in front of a crowd of 10,000 people while everybody laughs at her because of her accent. If this came true, it would make her feel as though she is a failure.

One time, Yoshi's sister crashed the car into a fence at home when he was learning how to drive. Yoshi's' maternal grandfather got angry at him, because he thought "How could you be so stupid?!" Yoshi's grandfather doesn't like Yoshi mowing the lawn, because he feels like he can't do it right. He will even stop Yoshi from mowing the lawn and do it himself, which Yoshi absolutely hates. It is obvious here that Yoshi's grandfather feels like a failure and is only projecting that feeling onto others.

EXAMPLE #2

Benjamin, a basketball coach, gets very nervous when he is coaching at games because he is afraid that he will have a panic attack in front of everybody. If he were to have a panic attack in front of others, he would fear that others would think he is weak and less of a man - essentially, incompetent.

Benjamin's father gets angry when others can't do things right. His worst-case scenario, is if he himself couldn't do anything right which would make him feel like a failure.

Benjamin's paternal grandmother experiences anxiety and worries if her son (Benjamin's uncle) will die because he does drugs. If he dies, it would make her feel like a failure.

EXAMPLE #3

Clayton does not like his girlfriend hanging out with one of her male employees that he does not like. As a result of the problems being stirred in his relationship, Clayton's girlfriend shares this with a business partner to discuss whether they should let go of this employee. Clayton gets angry at his girlfriend for sharing that with her business partner, because his worst fear is for all the employees within his girlfriend's company to find out about what he said. If they do, he is scared that they will all ridicule him, convincing his girlfriend to leave him. Above all, if this all came true, it would make him feel like he does not matter and that he does not exist.

Clayton first applies the P.E.W.F. process with his mom because he believes he has the most strained relationship with her. Not surprisingly, he finds that his mom also harbors feelings of not existing, which she conceals with anger. When, for example, Clayton is not able to take her somewhere because of time constraints, his mother feels like she does not matter.

Clayton works in the family business, and his father does not like him working on projects his father does not want him to be a part of, getting angry if he does so. His worst fear would be Clayton ruining his company to the ground. This is obviously how Clayton's father feels about himself, as his worst fear would be him ruining his own business to the ground. If his worst fear came true, it would make him feel he like a failure. I asked if Clayton ever experienced feelings of failure, to which he agreed, simultaneously trying to restrain the emotions coming to the surface.

EXAMPLE #4:

Theo is a high functioning autistic teenager who doesn't like to be interrupted when he is in the middle of something. He could be doing something as simple as playing a video game and if he is about to enter a master level and is suddenly interrupted by his mother, for example, he can completely lose it and get extremely angry.

His worst fear would be to work at a "crappy" retail job where everybody is ordering him around to do stuff constantly all at the same time, making him unable to get a single thing done. If this came true, it would make him feel like a failure.

Not surprisingly, Theo's mother is similar to her son in the sense that she doesn't like to be interrupted at work. She is a bilingual employee, so people are constantly interrupting her, by asking her for help. Her worst fear would be to have a major project at work and when it comes time for the deadline, she is unable to be complete it. This would make her feel like a failure.

Theo's father, who Theo describes as "overprotective," worries a lot about Theo's well-being. His father's worst fear would be Theo's death. If it came true, it would make him feel "useless" because he failed to protect him. Theo also experiences anxiety when he is late. He fears when he is late, something bad will happen to him, meaning he will unable to get to his responsibilities and will thus set him up to be a failure.

Interestingly, I too get frustrated when I am interrupted. There is an old gentleman who works at my father's pharmacy, where I rent an office space for my practice. He has to use my office everyday for a 30 minute nap. I'm already inundated with work and writing my book and I hate to be interrupted by him everyday while I'm working. Listening to Theo's experiences, I learned that frustration over being interrupted is projecting the blame of one's feelings of failure onto another.

EXAMPLE #5

Yolanda gets angry when she feels her friends are not supportive enough of her, because it makes her feel she does not matter. This feeling of not mattering comes from both of her parents. In fact, most of the time, Yolanda's mother bottles up her emotions (i.e. depression). For example, during the divorce, she never showed any signs of weakness or vulnerability. But, her bottled up emotions, from time to time, come to the surface and even explode out of control in the form of anger. One of the things she is most angry about is Yolanda's father not caring enough for his children. Yolanda's mother feels she does not matter and projects that feelings onto how her husband treats their children.

Yolanda's feelings of not mattering, with for example, her thinking her friends are not there for her enough, are really internalized from her mother. Before Yolanda would never confide with her friends, because as her mother would, she would present the facade and mask that everything is okay with her. Just more recently, Yolanda is learning to honor her true self by sharing her vulnerability and confiding with others, but Yolanda's friends just tell her she will be fine because they are so used to her mask of "everything is okay."

Yolanda's father experiences anger when the people he manages at work goof off or don't care. Everything has to be done his way. Even if his siblings were to have a social, political, or religious view that was remotely different than his own, he would want no part of it. His worst fear would be, not having the authority he is used to at work, and for everyone to not listen to him, which would make him feel he does not matter.

As you can see, Yolanda's father thinks he is always right, so much so that even when he is clearly wrong, he will never ever allow himself to admit it. His worst fear in this sense is to be wrong. If he is wrong, it will mean he is incompetent and thus, a failure. Yolanda also experiences feelings of incompetence when other people at work tell her she didn't do something the right way. She, like her father, also thinks she is always right. However, Yolanda's father's feelings of incompetence, the same ones she has internalized, actually come from his own mother. Namely, Yolanda's paternal grandmother experiences depression, especially when she sees Yolanda in emotional pain. Yolanda's grandmother's worst fear would be for Yolanda to always be in pain which would make her feel like a failure.

As this example suggests, Yolanda's father's feelings of incompetence stem from his mother. Yolanda's feelings of incompetence come not only from her father, but also her mother, as her mother's worst fear would be for her children to die before her, which would make her feel like a failure. It is evident that everyone here is just an emotional sponge to their parents' pain, especially because they all feel responsible for each other.

After applying the P.E.W.F. process to both yourself and your parents, you have likely experienced the revelation that you absorbed and internalized their feelings by making it yours. Now that you have recognized this truth, we will move on to the next stage of F.I.S.T., which is the "separation" from what does not belong to you.

PART TWO (F.I.S.T.)

Separation

Separation is drawing a healthy line in the sand, separating your space from the space of others.

```
        YOU    :    OTHER
```

"I DO NOT EXIST"

When other people's emotional "stuff" seeps into your space, they can no longer heal it because their stuff can only be healed in their space. More importantly, because you believe their emotional stuff is yours which makes you feel responsible for them, their emotional stuff consumes your entire personal space and spreads like a cancer. It prevents you from knowing your true self and, in turn, you cannot know your worth, leaving you feeling worthless and as if you don't exist.

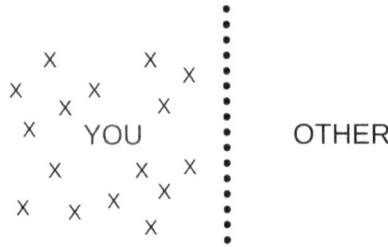

"I AM A FAILURE"

I have seen countless clients since I opened my practice in 2010, and the first and most recurring core pain that comes up in my clients' descriptions of their feelings reflects the phrase "I don't exist." If you dig deeper, the pain within that is "I am a failure." Since it is impossible to fix this pain you feel responsible for, because it does not belong to you, you feel you are a failure. You are essentially failing at fixing this pain that has consumed your whole existence, making you feel like a worthless failure who should not exist.

"Something is wrong with me"

The feeling of failure can also manifest as feeling "something is wrong with me." Holding onto the belief that "something is wrong with me," in turn, is holding onto a hopeless feeling of failure, because if you believe something is wrong with you, then there is absolutely nothing you can do about it. The truth is, it feels hopeless because it truly is hopeless, as you cannot fix what does not belong to you.

If we consider how this tendency reflects in our society, the obsession with attaining success at any cost and feeling like failures otherwise can be attributed back to the pain we unknowingly internalized from our parents and as a result, felt responsible for.

DO YOU FEEL RESPONSIBLE FOR OTHERS?

Ask yourself, do you feel responsible for others? If you do, describe how you act responsible for others here:

_____

_____

Example: "I feel responsible for my siblings. When something bad happens to them, I feel I failed them."

Codependency is feeling responsible for someone else, which is rooted in feeling responsible for the pain of our parents. However, because we cannot save what does not belong to us, our codependent selves will undoubtedly feel like a failure. Knowing this will actually help you let go of the feeling of failure. Feeling responsible for others wipes out your superpower and, ironically, eliminates your ability to help others *effectively*. Feeling responsible for other people allows all their emotional stuff to seep into and consume your entire personal space like cancer, preventing you from knowing your true self and leaving you feeling worthless and powerless.

You Are Spiderman

The reason why other people's feelings can easily seep into your space and thus feel like they belong to you, is because we were all were born with the gift of sensitivity. Sensitivity is what allows you to feel what others feel.

Ask yourself the following:

"Do you have an intuitive sense of how others feel?"

In other words, when others feel anxious, depressed or frustrated, are you able to sense it in them? If so, then you may be among the 1 out of 5 people born with the gift of high sensitivity. That means you can feel what others feel, like an X-ray.

You have the superpower of someone like Spiderman. Just as Spiderman can hear cries for help miles and miles away, you can strongly feel the pain of others. However, Spiderman can differentiate that these voices are the voices of other people while you, on the other hand, were born with the gift of sensitivity as a child, and had no idea you possessed it, causing you to feel the voices and feelings of others as if they were yours. Regardless, it is impossible to fix these voices (i.e. feelings) of others that you think are yours because it simply is that, not yours, which leaves you feeling like a hopeless failure.

E.S.C.

After you know these feelings do not belong to you, the question becomes how you go about clearing your space of all the negative feelings that consume you. First, you need not only to acknowledge that this pain does not belong to you, but also to constantly remind yourself that you are not responsible for this pain. Then, you need to take the following three steps of separation, which I call E.S.C. - to separate yourself from this pain.

Think of E.S.C., like the esc button (escape) on your keyboard. Imagine hitting the escape key on your keyboard, wiping out all the countless windows on your computer, representative of "pop-ups," or, other people's emotional stuff, allowing you to start anew to your true self.

1. **E**motional Antennas.

2. **S**.A.M.

3. **C**hanneling words of healing

CHAPTER 7 (E.S.C.)

❖

EMOTIONAL ANTENNAS

Every child is born with the gift of sensitivity, which means they were born into this world with emotional antennas. With this in mind, the feelings you carry now are only the emotional signals you picked up from your parents since you were that sensitive child. However, because nobody told you have these emotional antennas, you felt the pain of your parents as if it was yours.

EMOTIONAL ANTENNAS EXERCISE

Note: Children can and should perform this exercise.

1. Take an object weighing at least two pounds and place it on your lap.

2. Although this may seem a bit silly, for a few seconds, put your two index fingers pointing upward and put them on both sides of your head, as if they are your **emotional antennas**. (See image on next page) After you place your hands back down, know that your emotional antennas are always by the sides your head because you

were born with the gift of sensitivity and could feel what others feel.

3. Close your eyes, feel the weight on your lap, tap into that same core feeling (not existing, failure, etc) you identified earlier within yourself, and allow yourself to access the emotion you used to avoid feeling that core feeling (i.e.: anger, anxiety, depression)

4. Keep your eyes closed. Allow yourself to feel and recognize these feelings and emotions as the emotional signals you picked up through your emotional antennas from your parents when you were a child. The painful feelings you carry today originated from the pain you internalized from your parents.

CHAPTER 8 (E.S.C.)

❖

S.A.M.

Now that you know you are carrying the feelings of your parents as your own, a powerful mantra you can use to separate from this feeling is to remind yourself S.A.M.

SHIT AIN'T MINE!

If you want the PG version, you can use the mantra, STUFF AIN'T MINE. The purpose of this simple acronym is to affirm that the pain you feel is not yours. This creates a healthy line in the sand to honor your space and the space of others, namely your parents.

In a moment, I am going to have you say S.A.M. to all the feelings, emotional coping mechanisms and problems that do not belong to you. You are separating from these emotions because they are the coping mechanisms you internalized from your parents. Similarly, the reason why you are separating from "your" problems is because they are the manifestation of unknowingly mistaking your parents' pain for your pain while projecting it onto an external problem you falsely think is your own.

S.A.M. Exercise

List the following that you want to separate from using the S.A.M. exercise:

Feelings (the ones you thought were your own): ____

_____

Emotions / coping mechanisms (How you avoided those feelings): _____

_____

Take the same object you placed on your lap during the emotional antennas exercise into your hands, representing your parents' emotional stuff you internalized. As you are holding this object in your hands, really feel all your core feelings (i.e. "I'm a failure," "I don't exist.") and your emotions meant to mask those feelings (i.e. anger, anxiety, depression) all within that object. Now, say "S.A.M." to the object in your hands and imagine transferring it back into your parents' space by physically moving the object away from yourself, across the healthy line of separation and into their space. At the very same time, feel yourself separating from your parents' feelings and emotional coping mechanisms.

As you are physically moving the object of your parents' feelings back into their space, say outloud, "Shit ain't mine." (Note: Your children can perform this exercise with you and you can have them tell you "Stuff ain't mine....Here you go, I think you dropped something."

My Example: Declaring S.A.M. to "my" feelings of "I don't exist" and "I'm a failure," and my emotions of anger and anxiety meant to mask myself from feeling these feelings. Also, by simply saying S.A.M. to my parents' feelings, and everybody else's feelings I feel responsible for, empowers me because holding onto it as if it was mine, is what makes me feel like I'm a hopeless failure that should not exist.

BREATH OUT WHAT IS NOT YOURS

The final part of S.A.M. is to breathe out everything that does not belong to you. This is because S.A.M. signifies achieving a mental separation. Breathing out other people's emotional stuff cleanses your being and allows you to truly feel this separation, no longer identifying with the object that burdens and weighs you down.

Breathe Out What Is Not Yours [Exercise]

1. Be seated and close your eyes with your feet flat on the floor.

2. Take three deep breaths. With each breath out, breathe out everything that does not belong to you. Imagine you are blowing leaves out of your

front yard back into the space they fell from, as if you are a gardener clearing the leaves out of a yard.

3. Breathe out these feelings, emotional coping mechanisms and problems that do not belong to you. Breathe them outside of your personal space.

CHAPTER 9 (E.S.C.)

❖

CHANNELING WORDS OF HEALING

*"You are not an emotional sponge,
but a source of light."*

Now that you have placed your parents' emotional stuff back into their personal space, you can finally use your gift of sensitivity, because your parents' emotional stuff can only be healed in their space and not in your front yard. You will be using your gift of sensitivity the right way as a source of light and not as before like an emotional sponge.

It helps to use the analogy of the self as Superman. Like Kryptonite, which causes Superman's superpowers to vanish, feeling responsible for others, causes you to absorb and internalize all their pain as if it were your own. In other words, when you feel responsible for others, you internalize the pain of others which becomes the kryptonite that breaks you down physically, emotionally and mentally.

The more you take the kryptonite of feeling responsible for the burden of other people's feelings and hold onto it, coddle it, or even try to defeat it, as if it belongs to you, the more it covers you with a blanket of black tar that suffocates you to the point where you cannot breathe. In reality, this suffocating pain is impossible to fix, because it does not belong to you, which causes you to escape into a lifetime of hopeless depression, anxiety and anger. Moreover, when you fail at fixing this pain, which has consumed your entire existence, there is seemingly no reason to live -- a major contributing factor to feeling so helpless that something as drastic as suicide can feel like the only way out. Ultimately, as disheartening as this may feel, separation of what is not yours is the only salvation through which you can unlock your superpower.

Surrendering your responsibility for others allows you to use your gift to help others, because you are not an emotional sponge, but a source of light.

TWO STAGES OF CHANNELING:

There are two stages to channeling, with the second stage being more important. The first stage, is channeling the words of healing that your parents need to say in order to heal. Imagine and feel a beam of light flowing through you and into the souls of your parents. What I mean by "soul" is their higher self. If you tell their physical self, they will most likely not listen because their physical selves are still attached to their egos. But their higher selves are always receptive and will always listen

An example of what I channel to my parents' souls is: "You are infinitely loved," which combats the feeling of not existing and "You are perfect just the way you are," which combats the feeling that they are failures.

CHANNELING INSTRUCTIONS:

Words of healing you personally want to channel to your parents and grandparents: _____

_____

_____

Now, close your eyes and visualize these words like a beam of light flowing through you directly into their being and eventually reaching the generations before them.

(Children's version of channeling: Close your eyes and send a message to your parents with your mind and heart as if you are wishing upon a star.)

S.A.Y.

Moving along, the second stage of channeling, is what I call, S.A.Y., which stands for "Shit ain't yours!" I want you to channel the phrase "S.A.Y." to your inner child (where it all began for you), your parents and grandparents. Keep in mind that each generation is just unknowingly misusing their gift of sensitivity as an emotional sponge to their parents' feelings.

In order to channel S.A.Y. to them all, I want you to combine both S.A.M. and S.A.Y. together, by saying:

"Shit ain't mine! And, shit ain't yours either!"

Repeating these words recognizes the intergenerational cycle of pain and for once, puts an end to it by announcing "We are not an emotional sponge but a source of light." Much like the previous exercise where you lifted the heavy object off of your lap, you are going to now put it back in your hands and then place it in a designated space called "nowhere land," thereby removing the emotional burden for all of you. Doing this, allows you to feel and connect with how energetically powerful you truly are.

CHAPTER 10

❖

HEALTHY BOUNDARIES OF SEPARATION

A client once told me, "I feel if I channel words of healing to my parents, the words will just bounce right back because they will shut the door ." In fact, I asked the client how he responded when his parents would project their emotional stuff onto him and he said it would escalate into a verbal fight.

When one thinks of boundaries to "protect oneself" from the toxic feelings of others, it is typical to resort to:

1. Aggression by verbally fighting with others, or

2. Passively tuning them out, or passively complying with what others want them to do while sweeping their feelings under the rug.

The problem with falling into the habit of either making an aggressive cut off or wall to shut someone out, or passively tuning them out and complying, you still absorb their pain. This happened to me, as my mom would often project her feelings onto me with the fear of not existing by obsessing to me over health and safety. I used to fight with her to make her stop. It always resulted in the two of us talking over each other, leading me to simply tune her out as she was nagging, with my father as the referee. I learned if I were to say how I truly felt, it would set her off, like a ticking time bomb, making matters even worse. In an effort to prevent an explosion, I became conditioned to keep my mouth shut and just let her say whatever she wanted. Unbeknownst to me, however, I was still freely absorbing all of my mom's feelings.

In order to stop absorbing the feelings of others, I invite you to practice a "loving no." When people try to put their toxic feelings into your space, simply call them out and tell them to stop projecting their emotional stuff onto your space. You do not need to fight with them. It's just a loving "no," to honor the healthy boundary of separation that protects your space and theirs, just like that line in the sand.

Although it is tempting, it is important not to engage with them on the level of their toxic logic and reasoning. If they claim that you don't care about them, because, for example, they feel they don't matter, or they put you down in some way, because they feel like a failure, do not try to prove them wrong. In essence, they are putting their emotional stuff into your space and you are finally creating a healthy boundary by saying a "loving no" and telling them you will not ac-

YOU ARE THE F*CKING SH*****T

cept someone projecting their emotional stuff into your space. Just a fair warning: they will go berserk, because projecting their feelings onto you is how they avoid feeling them. But you must stay firm in this healthy boundary you have drawn in order to respect both your personal space and the personal space of others.

Here is a scenario using myself as an example to illustrate the immense power of the loving no and healthy boundaries. When my mother obsessively nags at me about health and safety, I know she feels responsible for me and that my death would make her feel like a failure. In response, I respond by saying: "You are not responsible for me." Also, when she tells me if I don't care for her enough, I tell her "you matter….but these feelings of not existing do not belong to me." All of these responses are far better than engaging with her faulty logic or passively ignoring her.

Once you engage with other people's toxic level of reasoning by, for example, proving them wrong and proving why you are right, you have immediately allowed them to dump their emotional stuff onto your space. Although you might believe that you can change them by engaging with their toxic logic rooted in the projection of their pain, remember that their stuff can only be healed in their space. You are only enabling them. They find themselves projecting their stuff onto your space because it's a temporary escape to avoid feeling their pain. But just as you, and all of us, they are carrying pain that does not belong to them, but to their parents. Ultimately, you do not want to engage with their toxic level of reasoning because it can only hurt them knowing that this pain they are projecting belongs to their parents and is not even theirs to begin with.

I understand it may be difficult to set up a boundary with others, especially with your parents, whom you subconsciously feel responsible for. In spite of the challenge, setting up a loving boundary requires letting go of this both false and impossible responsibility for others, liberating both you and them.

What people say or do to put their feelings into your space: _____

_____

How you respond which permits others to put their emotional stuff into your space:

_____

_____

What you will do differently to honor your personal space and theirs: _____

_____

There is a good chance that in spite of your loving boundaries, the other person will respond by becoming defensive, choosing to be in denial, or continuing the behavior. Regardless, this is your chance to mindfully separate from the energies of their feelings by telling yourself their emotional stuff is not yours. You are no longer the emotional sponge to the unhealed pain of others. You are a source of light. Having said that, you still want to continue to be firm by maintaining your loving boundaries. Almost immediately, it will fundamentally change the dynamic of your interaction because you are no longer going to fall into the black tar pits of their projection of pain onto your space.

Example: Clayton's father doesn't want him working on certain projects for the family business. If he does, it makes his father angry. Clayton's father does this because he believes Clayton is incapable of handling it and doesn't want him to "ruin" the company as a result. All that Clayton's father is doing is projecting his feelings of failure onto Clayton. Clayton responds to his father's anger about working on projects his father thinks he shouldn't be involved with by just timidly saying "okay" and going along with it. Without a healthy boundary in place, Clayton also, in turn, feels intense feelings of failure. However, when these situations arise, Clayton will need to tell his father a "loving no" and remind his father that these are his feelings that have nothing to do with him.

CHAPTER 11

❖

RELATIONSHIPS: HEALTHY BOUNDARIES IS A TWO-WAY STREET

(Note: this section does not just pertain to couples, but applies to all forms of relationships where both sides are really butting heads with each other.)

Relationships will, often, by default, setup both partners to trigger each other's core pain. For instance, my fiancée's greatest fear is to be out of control, internalized from her father, which causes her to constantly be in hyper planning mode. If something is left unplanned or in her eyes unknown, it makes her feel anxious, becoming the driving force for her compulsive desire to plan. She plans our weekends, months and year in advance. Furthermore, if things are not done a certain way or according to her plan, she feels as though she does not matter. Even if one minor detail within her plan is remotely changed by someone else,

YOU ARE THE F*CKING SH*****T

it makes her anxious and even angry at times, because her existence feels dependent upon it.

She often randomly presents something to me out of the blue and wants me to make a decision on it right away. Her fear of the unknown makes her so uncomfortable that she will misinterpret me simply listening to what she is saying as a confirmed yes, assuming that I am in agreement. It has reached the point where I require my fiancée to email me her requests where nothing is confirmed until I respond "read and agreed."

I know I may be painting my fiancée as some demon, but she is beyond loving and caring to me. However, this incessant desire to overplan, can often be misinterpreted by me as selfishness and everything having to be her way, which automatically makes me implode with anger because it also triggers my core pain of "I don't matter." By responding to my fiancée's overplanning with explosive anger, however, it destroys all possibility of civil communication and catapults the two of us into an emotional frenzy.

I have since understood that it's not that she is being selfish but rather, that she is just overplanning to avoid her fear of being out of control and the feeling like she does not matter. As a result, I remind myself not to overreact to her overplanning with my anger of

"I don't matter." By removing my emotional coping mechanism of anger, I can see her behavior as a way to avoid pain and not as a part of some selfish demon, allowing us to be able to come to the table and communicate calmly and lovingly.

To give you an example, I often give into my fiancée planning most of our weekend time together. One Sunday, we did everything according to her plans; we went to the museum, although I do not like museums. Afterwards, we took two hours to go walking around Downtown LA. After eating dinner, she had planned for us to go to a coffee shop so the both of us could do our work. I did not want to go to the coffee shop she selected because it was out of the way on our way back home. I wanted to have as much time at the coffee shop to do our work, as it was already getting late. Because I wanted to change the location of the coffee shop, my fiancée got both anxious and angry, which automatically made me furious because I was thinking I had spent the whole day doing what she had planned and all I wanted to do was change the location of the coffee shop.

After a period of both of us letting out our steam, I reminded myself that it's not that she is selfish, but is really being overprotective with her planning to avoid the feeling of not mattering. I removed my emotion of anger, which was my coping mechanism, to avoid my feeling of not mattering. Afterward, I more calmly communicated how I only intended to change the location to something closer to home, and that I had already attended all the activities that she had planned for us. This calm way of communication, void of the anger whose purpose is to protect my feeling of not mattering, was able to reach her to where she could see how she was being overprotective with her planning to avoid the feeling of not mattering.

Relationships are often going to be like this, meaning that often times, you will be each other's emotional landmines - either with your partners, family members or other loved ones. I want you to let go of your emotional coping mechanisms whose purpose is to avoid having you feel your core pain. Furthermore, see how the other person is only acting out of pain and isn't the evil demon that you make them out to be. Your knee jerk reaction to their overreaction is you acting of out of your pain. You will be better off if you remove the pain of your feelings and emotions from the equation and come to the table with your partner so you communicate calmly and lovingly.

THE TWO WAY STREET EXERCISE:

The other person's behavior that bothers you: _____

_____

Their core pain (i.e: "I don't matter") underlying their behavior: _____

_____

Your core pain triggered by their behavior: _____

_____

MY EXAMPLE:

The other person's behavior that bothers you: My fiancée has to always have things her way

Their core pain underlying their behavior: Overplanning to avoid the feeling of being out of control, which brings up feelings of not mattering

Your core pain triggered by their behavior: My fiancée's overplanning makes me feel as though I don't matter.

I advise you to see the other person's core pain underneath their behavior while acknowledging and removing your core pain being triggered by that behavior. Communicate without your emotional coping mechanisms (i.e. anger, anxiety) and speak to acknowledge the core pain within both of you. Afterwards, you two can calmly communicate what you originally wanted to discuss without the landmines of each other's core pain being in the way.

NARCISSISM = CODEPENDENCY

One of the most common problems we experience in relationships that signifies how all relationships are a two way street is the conflict between narcissism and codependency. The truth is they are not in conflict of each other but truly mirror each other.

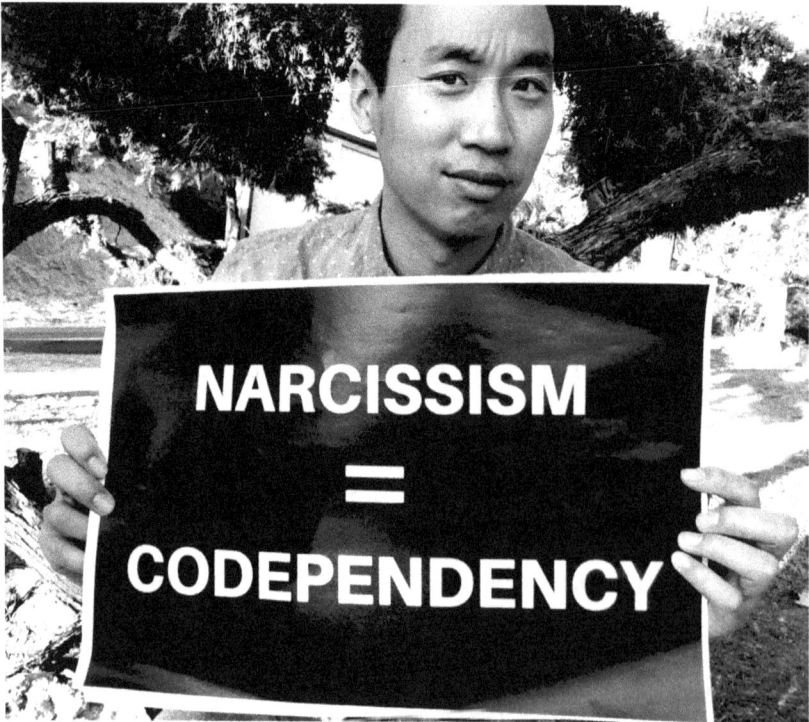

As shocking or ludicrous as this statement may sound, there is nothing that distinguishes narcissism from codependency. Narcissists want to have things their way because if they do not get their way, they will feel they do no matter. Their feeling of not mattering was the feeling they internalized from their parents and thus feel responsible for. Feeling responsible for others is codependency. Understanding this will often help you and especially in your conflicts with other people that you find "selfish," because you now know the "selfish" person is only acting out of their parents' pain that they feel responsible for. You, likewise, in getting angry over the person you find selfish, stems from you projecting the blame of your parents' pain of not mattering, in which you feel responsible for, onto the other person.

"Letting go of the responsibility for others is letting go of all your pain."

Or in other words:

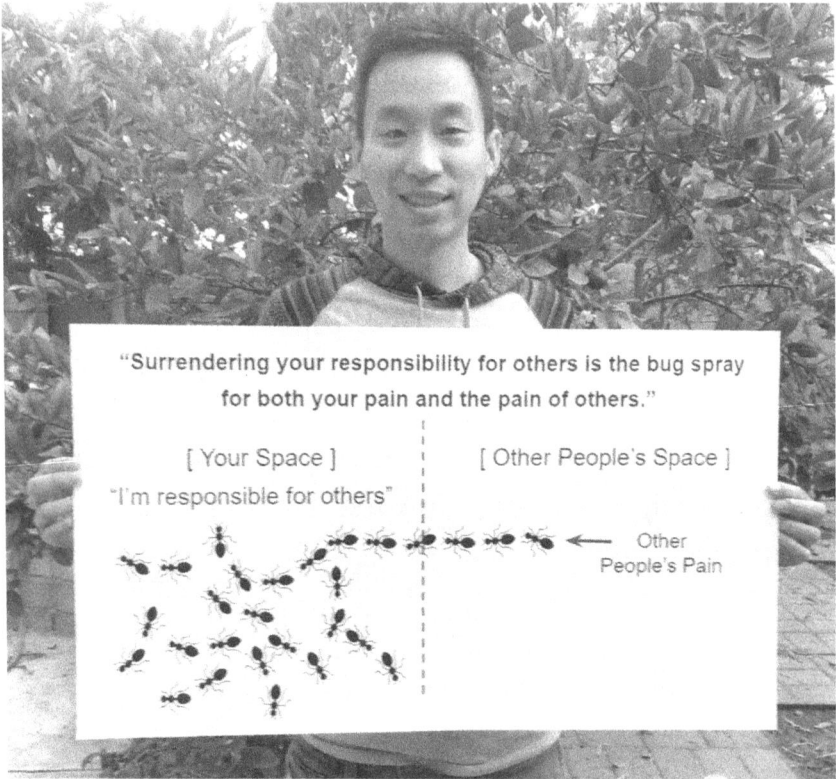

Feeling responsible for others, invites an ant infestation of their feelings into your personal space. The ants of their feelings consumes your entire space to the point where you do not know who you are. "Their pain" has become "your pain" and essentially, your identity. All because you believe you are responsible for them.

On top of that, it is impossible to heal what is not yours, which inevitably makes you feel like a hopeless failure.

For example, when your loved ones don't listen to your suggestive words to benefit them (or when you verbally fight with them and they just simply don't listen). It drives you over the edge, because you feel not only responsible for them, but at the same time you feel helpless when they do not listen to you. Since their actions make you feel like a helpless failure, and you can often take your anger (feelings of failure) out on them by making them feel like a failure for not being able to take care of themselves.

I see this phenomenon in my personal life, as my mom feels responsible for me, and I, in turn, feel responsible for my fiancée. One day my fiancée was not feeling well and so she binged on the internet until 5 in the morning. She woke up a few hours later and went back onto the internet. Her foot fell asleep while using her laptop on the couch, and when she got up from the couch, she tripped and hurt her ankle badly. We both thought that she had fractured her ankle (luckily X-rays showed it was just a sprain) because she could not put any weight on it and it was swollen like a tennis ball. As I was taking her to urgent care, I was so angry at her, because I felt that the accident was a consequence of her failure to take care of herself. More importantly, I felt like a helpless failure because no matter what I say, she does not listen to me. Still, I did take out my feelings of failure onto her by angrily telling how she simply cannot take care of herself.

Like the example above, your false responsibility for others also can explain why it is so challenging to assert yourself and set boundaries with others when they put their emotional stuff into your space. Although you believe they are your responsibility, this can change by considering the following:

Only when you surrender your responsibility for others can you not only heal your pain but begin offer the same healing to others. Take a moment now and think of all your feelings, emotions and "problems" (which are really how you make other people's pain your everyday living reality) and then recite the statement here:

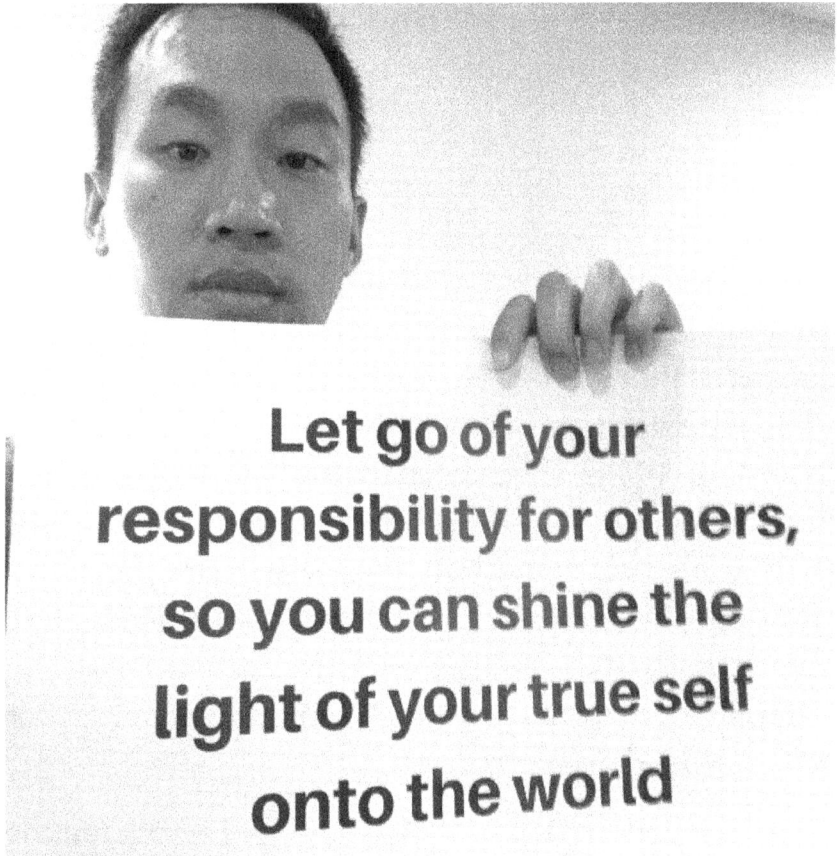

Let go of your responsibility for others, so you can shine the light of your true self onto the world

EXAMPLE #1:

Nora often experiences anger due to problems in her marriage. Her worst fear would be getting a divorce and having her son suffer tremendously because of it, which would make her feel like a failure, or in her words, "the worst mother in the world." Similarly, if Nora were to do something to disappoint her mother (i.e. divorce), it would make her feel like a failure herself, because Nora's mother's worst fear would be-ing completely incapable of fixing or undoing Nora's wrongs.

Nora's father gets angry when Nora's mother doesn't do things his way, which could be something as simple and seemingly silly as what kind of fruit to buy. His worst fear would be nothing going his way, which would make him feel as though he does not matter. Nora finds it diffi-cult that her feelings belong to her parents, so I ask about her grandparents. Nora reveals that, much like her fa-ther, her paternal grandfather gets angry when things don't go his way. He is very controlling, and he owns a family business where everybody within the family must listen to him, or else. His worst-case scenario would be his family betraying him, which would lead him to con-clude that he does not matter.

I then, in turn, asked Nora if she experiences feelings of not mattering, and she describes a time when her and her husband were about to go to have dinner with friends, but Nora suddenly felt uneasy, as she was 6 months pregnant at the time. Although Nora had giv-en her husband the freedom to go out without her, but because he actually did go on without her, she went into a rage and ended up demanding a divorce. The reason why she was so angered was because him leav-ing her alone brought up feelings of not mattering, which mind you, were feelings she originally internalized from her father.

While Nora is going through all of this emotionally, Nora's husband feels helpless in trying to rescue Nora from her feelings. He does everything she says, but still, she gets angry at him. He tells Nora that he feels like he is walking on eggshells in this marriage, which is indicative of how he feels responsible for how she feels. Not surprisingly, when Nora gets angry at him, despite all his efforts to please her, it makes him feel useless. Interestingly, just as in the relationship between Nora and her husband, Nora's husband's father also tries to do everything he can to appease his wife and gets anxious when his wife yells at him for doing things "wrong" by not doing it her way.

As the patterns in this example suggest, it is apparent that virtually everybody is feeling responsible for each other, which only causes a cesspool of pain and suffering for all. Moving forward, Nora's goal is to not push her emotional feelings of not mattering into her husband's space, which in essence, is making her husband responsible for her. Moreover, she must remind her husband that he is not responsible for her feelings, especially when he is attempting to do everything he can to emotionally save in her what he could not save in his own parents.

EXAMPLE #2:

Cindy feels neglected by her mother because she feels she isn't there for her emotionally. Cindy remembers one instance during her childhood, when she fell and she felt emotionally neglected by her mother, because although her father gave her a hug to comfort her, her mother hurriedly just gave a bandaid and some medicine.

Although it may seem like Cindy's mother is not loving toward her, this is not the case, but rather reflects how Cindy's mother feels responsible for her. Cindy's mother's worst fear would be her daughters dying before her, which would make her feel like a failure. Cindy and her sister are the only reason why her mother lives on and chooses not to commit suicide. Since Cindy's mother feels responsible for her, all that she can think about is whether Cindy is safe, when will she be home, or in other words, "where's the bandaid?!"

Rightfully so, Cindy is only seeking the medicine of love from her mother. However, if Cindy can see that her mom is just acting out of the pain of false responsibility for her, instead of taking it to heart, then she can see that her mom is not neglecting her, but only neglecting herself emotionally, by sacrificing her soul in order to hold herself responsible for others.

SUMMARY FOR "SEPARATE"

1. Practice E.S.C. to separate from what does not belong to you:

   a. Emotional antennas: Feel your emotional antennas that have been picking up the emotional signals of your parents since you were a child.

   b. S.A.M.: Say "shit ain't mine" to all that does not belong to you (emotions, feelings and problems). Afterwards, breathe out all that does not belong to you, out of your being and space, to allow yourself to really feel this separation of what is not yours.

   c. Channeling: Channel words of healing to your parents and then channel S.A.Y. to your inner child, parents and the generations before them, by saying "Shit ain't mine and shit ain't yours either!"

2. Healthy boundaries of separation:

   a. Practice responding with a loving no, or boundary, to others, namely your parents, who put their emotional stuff into your space.

   b. Healthy boundaries is a two way street. See the core pain that is driving the other person's actions, as well as your core pain, which their actions are triggering. Let go of your emotional coping mechanisms (i.e. anger, anxiety) and speak to acknowledge the core pain within both of you. Afterwards, you can calmly communicate what you wanted to discuss without each other's core pain being in the way.

c. Surrendering your responsibility for others is the bug spray for both your pain and the pain of others.

PART THREE (F.I.S.T.)

TRUE SELF

After you finally separate from all that does not belong to you, you will begin to know and feel the power of your true self. Your true self is your source of light, peace, wisdom, power and love. It is your connection to your creator; God, love, Universe, or whatever divine or spiritual force you identify with.

To embody the power of your true self, there are four steps, which I call **P.U.M.A.** Think of the puma animal which signifies the balance of power and grace while going after what it wants.

1. **P**: Power

2. **U**: Unwavering belief.

3. **M**: Mode of being - continuously expressing your true self, no matter what

4. **A**: Action makes it a part of your being.

❖

POWER

"P" is the power of your true self which is the power of your king and queen self. Take a moment now to close your eyes and feel the power of your king and queen self. Feel the crown on your head. The power you feel within yourself is the power of your true self and the power of love who created you. Feel the power of your true self, whose light is unstoppable.

THE POWER OF FEELING

A lot of our power is derived from the act of feeling but we can often find ourselves consumed with our minds, which leads to me asking you the question:

DO YOU OVERTHINK A LOT?

We are always operating from our minds by constantly thinking and doing. As important as thoughts and actions are, however, they are only half the equation. Thoughts and actions are your ship to help you get to your destination. Feeling is your captain, as in the act of feeling. Without a captain, your ship will end up like the Titanic. At its core, then, thoughts and actions are about power. With "feeling" as your captain, you can synergistically combine both feeling and power by "feeling powerfully." Take a moment to close your eyes and access the yin and yang balance of feeling powerfully, thereby commanding your ship.

FEELING IS HEALING

As you are feeling powerfully, tell yourself, "feeling is healing" as it connects you to love. Even when you are feeling your uncomfortable feelings, it is feeling pain that gives pain the love it needs to heal. Pain is not your enemy. Pain is simply a wound needing the medicine of love to be nurtured. Avoiding your pain, then, only causes it to grow deeper and become so embedded within you that it is all consuming. You can even imagine the pain as an inner child who is hurt. You would not want to leave this hurt child alone. Their pain needs to be acknowledged and validated with love.

TO FEEL IS TO HEAL
FEELING PAIN
HEALS PAIN BECAUSE
FEELING IS HOW WE
CONNECT TO LOVE

HEAL
FROM THE GROUND UP

"HOW TO FEEL?"

When I asked one client to "feel powerfully," she responded with great difficulty in trying to perform the act of feeling powerfully, and then finally asked me, "How do you do that?" This is a clear example of how the mind is always trying to mentally make sense of the "how." What you really need, however, is simply to feel. Asking "how do you feel?" is like asking "how do you breathe?" You do not need to think about it, you just do it. After all this, if you are still having difficulty, you can connect with the act of feeling, by reminding yourself, "feeling is healing," as it connects you to love.

ALLOWING YOURSELF TO FEEL

After you learn the importance of feeling, the question is do you even allow yourself to feel? We are always so busy and on the go, constantly thinking and doing, without having any breaks within this hoopla of constant activity. I noticed this within myself. In fact, given that I'm busy going about my everyday life and pursuing my life goals, as important as they may be, I don't allow myself to take any breaks. What I consider a break is really just browsing youtube, social media, or watching television. I never allow myself a moment to just simply "feel." I'm scared that if I stop doing or thinking, for even a moment, then I will have to feel the pain of feeling like a failure, or feeling that I don't exist. However, not pausing the reset button for a moment during the day to simply feel, prevents you from connecting to love. Feeling is what grounds you and connects you to love. Whatever you are doing, do not rush through it. Allow yourself to be present, allow yourself to feel, and allow yourself to just be. I understand you may be very busy, but I urge you, to take moments throughout the day, and just allow yourself to feel, and to feel powerfully. Ultimately, the experience of simply feeling will be so transformative that it will center you, ground you, and make you one with love.

EXAMPLE OF OVERTHINKING:

I would like to now share an example of a client of mine, to show how overthinking can prevent you from knowing your core feelings and your core self. When I asked him to assign a specific percentage to capture the extent to which he identifies as a thinker, he said he was an 80% thinker and 20% feeler, who doesn't really know how to feel. In the very beginning of the first session, in fact, he told me he actually has no problems in his life and just wanted to protect himself in the event that a problem were to arise in the future. I asked him what he normally feels and he responded by sharing that he feels "optimism," which interestingly is a mindset and not a feeling. He also noted that he has difficulty giving empathetic advice to his friends who are going through tough times because he himself speaks to logic and removes emotion from his being, even if it pertains to the problems of others. For example, a friend could be going through a breakup and he would in a sense, dismiss their feelings, nonchalantly suggesting that they could just move on and be logical instead of being hurt or emotional about the situation.

I try to get to his core feelings and ask what situations bring up the strongest feelings in him, to which he responds that he is a rather happy person and never feels sad and feels most happy when he is around friends. I then proceed to ask him what he feels when he is not around friends and he answers, "lonely." There you go! Underneath all the over thinking and layers of logic, is the feeling of loneliness, meant to prevent him from feeling.

When I asked my client what his worst fear would look like, he said it would be having no friends and being alone and surprisingly, becoming homeless. If his worst fear were to come true, not only would it make him feel like he doesn't exist but also, that he would be a failure. He then reasoned that his fear of having no job and potentially ending up homeless would come true, confirming that he was a failure. Moreover, he internalized these feelings from his parents, as his parents also feel they would be failures if they were to lose their job and be unable to provide.

My client is an example to remind yourself to not lose yourself with over thinking but to balance your thoughts and actions with the act of feeling, by commanding your ship and "feeling powerfully"

THE MENTAL ABYSS

Ultimately, your mind and over thinking will plunge you into a deep abyss, with no end and no solution in sight. Over thinking only enables you in avoiding your painful feelings. If you avoid your feelings, you will never identify them, and they will control you for the rest of your life. As much as your mind may want to lead you astray, always practice the P.E.W.F. process (Problem – Emotion – Worst fear – Feeling about the Self). Its purpose is for you to be able to identify your feelings, which in turn will prevent your feelings from controlling you in an unhealthy way.

CHAPTER 13 (P.U.M.A.)

❖

UNWAVERING BELIEF

"U" is the unwavering belief that you can do anything. It is the belief that you can do it, you will do it, and you are doing it! It is knowing that your light is unstoppable. In short, it is telling yourself:

"I got this shit!"

Or, if you want to the PG version, you can say,
"I got this!"

I had knee surgery over 15 years ago and I never was really ever able to rehab it correctly. I've seen many physical therapists and massage therapists over the years to help me work on my chronically tight muscles and strained muscles. I didn't walk correctly as there was a little bit of a hitch in my walk. The left side of my body sat lower than my right because my left knee wasn't fully straightened when I either would stand or walk. I went to a new sports massage therapist recently and she noticed that my right leg had a lot more muscle than my left leg where the surgery was performed on. She evaluated my left knee and said it was fine and felt that my leg issues were stemming from my mind. She concluded that I was protecting my knee as I was walking in order not to hurt it. The reason why I subconsciously did not straighten my left leg while I was standing or walking was in order to protect my knee. As such, this overprotective way of walking caused me to walk incorrectly, leading to tight and strained muscles. Coincidentally, this example reflects the metaphor for avoiding pain and feeling by protecting ourselves with those emotional coping mechanisms I referred to earlier. Still, much like my physical manifestation of pain, avoidance leads to more pain.

In the back of my mind, I was scared that my leg would just get worse and that I would end up having to use a walker at an early age and eventually have such poor health that I would be confined to a wheelchair or be bedridden. This would mean that I would not function, not be productive, become a failure who does not exist, and ultimately, die. To recap, if my health was so poor that I was rendered useless, I would feel like a failure who should not exist, all of which reflect the feelings I absorbed from my parents. Further, the massage therapist's insight that I was over-protecting my knee brought to the surface my coping mechanism of trying to avoid the pain I absorbed to prevent becoming a useless human being. Ever since she suggested that I should walk freely and powerfully, I have been able to do things physically with my legs that I thought I was could never do again. As a result, I now tell myself that I do have a healthy body and that I can walk normally and powerfully. Upon seeing my physical therapist only a week later, he wanted to see my progress with how I was walking. As I was walking for him, I kept telling myself silently in my head, "I got this shit!" After seeing me walk, my physical therapist told me my gait had improved tremendously. Above all else, this experience taught me to have the unwavering belief that I can accomplish whatever is in front of me, because after all, it was only my negative mindset that was creating my previous reality.

"I GOT THIS SHIT!" EXERCISE:

Where in your life are you lacking self-belief? Bring it up and completely transform your mindset about it by telling yourself "I got this shit!" Feel your power that can accomplish anything you set out to and overcome whatever challenge is in front of you. Pick up that crown, place it back on your head where it belongs, and tell yourself, "I can do it, I will do it, and I am doing it," and once again, "I got this shit!"

What do you want to say "I got this shit!" to?: _____

_____

_____

_____

CHAPTER 14 (P.U.M.A.)

❖

MODE OF BEING

When I asked a client what they believed would be the most important action they could take to honor their true self, they said that joining the navy as service to their country was very important to them. What I mean by the phrase "mode of being" is that it is not limited to a specific action or a period of time, but mode of being is shining the light of your true self at all times in all places, because it is who YOU are. Your greatest gift to humanity is YOU. The question is, how do you define your true self?

DEFINE THE ESSENCE OF YOUR TRUE SELF

Now that you can feel the power of your true self, I want you to define your true self in two separate words, as they support each other like a yin and yang. Your true self is your source of light, peace, wisdom, joy, power and love. For example, mine is playfulness and calmness. which I call "playful calmness"

Here is an example of something that reflects me living out my true self. I love to share my message with humanity as a whole, so I went to a political convention a few months back. Everybody was chanting the names of various politicians obsessively and I went around with a sign saying "Politicians are not your savior, you are!" I interviewed people with my fiancée as my camerawoman.

To give you an example of the fervor at this event and my playful response to it, one gentleman saw my sign and approached me by angrily asking me, "Are you an anarchist?!", to which I playfully responded to, "No, I'm a lovist!" This was the first time I ever brought my playful self and my calm intuitive self together, making me feel alive and free.

(Note: It helps to think of a time in your life where you felt the most alive, free, powerful, joyful or at peace. Afterwards, think of how you would best describe what feelings it brought up about who you are in one word.)

Define the first half of your essence in a word:

_____

REMEMBER, COMPASSION IS NOT YOUR ESSENCE

Keep in mind that people tend to define their true selves in terms of who they are in relation to other people.

This includes descriptions such as being compassionate, kind, caring, healing, and honest, to name a few. Although all of these attributes are important, helping others is only the after effect of your true self and not the means. If being compassionate is your essence then when you are alone in a room, you will feel you are not good enough, because you have to do something for others in order to feel whole. You want to be able to still feel the power of your true self when you are alone in a room while doing and thinking nothing because you who you just as you are is your greatest gift to humanity.

Like I put it earlier, the overwhelming majority of my clients typically repeatedly identify their true selves in terms of "we" (i.e. kindness, compassionate, service to others) over and over again, despite me explaining multiple times and in different ways how the essence of their true selves cannot be defined in relation to others. However, the real reason why people identify their true selves so strongly in terms of "we" is because of the false responsibility they hold for others.

Remember, it is not only impossible to be responsible for others, but making the pain of others your responsibility is one of the greatest causes of all pain. More importantly, identifying your true self in terms of "we" robs yourself and the world of your greatest gift, because it is the "me" that is your greatest gift to the "we.

Simply put, who you are is the greatest gift to humanity, but you must first know who you are, not in relation to others, to know your source of light.

If you defined your essence in relation to others, first breathe out all that does not belong to you, and then try again to define the essence of who you are here:

While it can be frustrating and challenging to define who you are outside of how it relates to those around you, taking the time to identify your true essence, which is the source of YOUR light, is an imperative part of the healing process. In fact, I remember one time, when I asked a client to define his true self, to which he responded with a long and painful period of silence. Being that I had already told him to not define his true self in relation to others, he felt helplessly lost, because all that his mind could possibly think of, were words like "compassionate," "kind" and "caring." It deeply pained him because he felt incapable of defining his true self, which made him feel that he did not exist. His whole life was dedicated to the servitude of others. What's more, this complete abandonment of himself was simultaneously manifesting in his body, in the form of a thyroid problem, as the thyroid is our center of self-expression (i.e. where you honor your voice).

The emotional pain that was blocking him, as well as his thyroid, was his false sense of responsibility for others. Consequently, I urged him to declare the following statement:

"I surrender my responsibility for others in order to shine the light of my true self onto the world."

If you feel at lost in trying to define your true self, not in relation to others, let this be an eye opener for you in how enmeshed your self-identity is with the pain of others. This will serve you in seeing how important it is to surrender your responsibility for others, so you can begin to honor the power and beauty of your true self.

PAIN = ESSENCE

People also often define their true selves with the pain they internalized from their parents. For example, I had a client tell me "anger" was the essence of her true self, when anger was only the coping mechanism that her father used to mask his pain of not existing when he did not get things his way.

Other examples of clients defining their true selves with their parents' pain were "productivity" and "competitiveness," which were examples of people combatting the feeling of failure they internalized from their parents. This dramatically shows that their parents' pain is so deeply embedded in them that they mistake it as their true identity.

We can even find ourselves seeking out the feeling of worthlessness, failure or not mattering, because we've internalized our parents' feelings to the point where we feel it is our burden alone to bear. One client told me she would purposely push her friends away because she wanted to feel worthless. Ask yourself, why do you often catch yourself self-sabotaging yourself and carrying out the very behavior you know causes your pain and suffering? It is because you seek it out since this is the only way your younger self knew how to help your parents.

If you chose your parents' pain as your essence, include it here: _____

_____

WORDS OF EMPOWERMENT

Remember, when you are finding the word that defines your essence, you should find a word that gives you a feeling of empowerment. For example, clients have defined their true selves to me as "open," as in wanting to experience new things. As such, a word of empowerment could be something like "explorer."

What really helps to find the word which defines your true self is to do the following: after you think of one word, ask yourself what that word means to you and why you were drawn to it. Next, describe a situation of yourself that depicts the feeling of this word. Afterwards, ask yourself what empowering feelings this situation brings up in you. For example, one client defined her true self as "independent." When I asked her what she meant by "independent," she said that she enjoys her time being home alone. Moreover, the feeling that being home alone brings up is being "grounded."

1. Think of one word that defines the essence of your true self = (i.e.:independent)

2. Describe a situation that depicts what that word means to you = (i.e.:enjoys being home alone)

3. What feelings does "enjoying your time home alone" give you? = (i.e.:grounded)

OTHER EXAMPLES:

1. Nancy relishes challenges. Once she was hiking on a mountain with friends and it got dark all of the sudden while they were lost. Her friends panicked, but she was relishing in it → Adventurer.

2. Franklin feels "comfortable" because he is at peace with all that he has → tranquility. For Franklin's second half of his true self, he describes as feeling powerful and very ambitious → Conqueror. Putting the two together we came up with → "Unstoppable Tranquility"

3. Jenny likes the peace she feels when she is in solitude → peaceful. The word "Warrior" is for the power she feels within herself that never gives up and sees things through → The Peaceful Warrior.

4. Dennis enjoys creating changes that establishes a new way of doing things → Trailblazer

If you chose a word that doesn't feel empowering, think of one here: _____
_____

After you have found a word that truly defines the first half of your true self, I want you to take a moment to feel the power of it. For example, if you identified yourself as the "explorer," take some time to feel the power of your explorer self by visualizing and feeling it now.

NAME THE SECOND HALF OF YOUR TRUE SELF

After you name one half, name the other half of your true self. Remember, they support each other, as yin and yang. One half is often lively, free, joyful and the other half can be grounding and calm.

The name of the second half of your true self: _____

_____

After you think of the two separate words that define your essence, combine the two into a single identity. As I mentioned before, mine is playfulness and calmness, which I identify as "Playful Calmness." Some other ones I have heard before are below:

1. Unstoppable Tranquility

2. The Silent Clown

3. The Quiet Goofball

4. Quirky Calmness

5. The Peaceful Spartan

6. Goofy Serenity

7. The Peaceful Explorer

8. The Zenful Trailblazer

The Name of Your True Self: (Note: the adjectives you employ to describe yourself, like those above, should not reflect who you are in relation to others) _____

_____

Take a moment now to close your eyes and feel the power of your true self (i.e. The Peaceful Explorer). Remember, this is your source of light and power, so you will want to shine the light of your true self at all times and in all places because it is who you are. Your true self is the beam of light that radiates, heals and empowers your loved ones and the world. Anytime you feel hopeless or powerless, put on the superman cloak of your true self and feel yourself becoming so elevated that you could fly.

CHAPTER 15 (P.U.M.A.)

❖

ACTION

Since action is the only way to manifest your new vision of healing, you must tap into your feelings but follow through by acting on them. You want to feel it, believe it and then act upon it.

What is the most important action you can take right now to honor your true self?

_____

_____

_____

_____

My Example: As I am writing this book, I constantly feel anxiety and hopelessness as I fear I will fail. The most important action for me now, is to focus on my unwavering self-belief, and keep staying on the path of my true self and not the actions of avoidance, like watching TV or browsing social media. By taking action and feeling powerfully, I can shift my mindset to look like this: My book will be an international bestseller that will transform humanity.

Repeat the Routine

Action is also about, what I call, "repeating the routine." What I mean by "repetition" is making F.I.S.T. a part of your everyday reality, which is like going to the gym. For all of your life, you have been working the muscle of "other people's pain is my responsibility." Now, you want to relinquish that muscle and work the muscle of your true self.

Making F.I.S.T. a routine is like brushing your teeth. Every morning, I want you to apply the process of F.I.S.T., because normally when we wake up, we feel anxious, frustrated and depressed with how hopelessly behind we are with all the things we need to do. The emotional strength of F.I.S.T. is not a destination, but rather, a way of life. Above all, emotional strength is about using your gift of sensitivity the right way and honoring the power of your true self. It is the very oxygen you breathe.

Think of it this way: does Superman find it a pain to use his superpower to be able to fly through the sky? Does Spiderman say, "Darnit! I have to yet again leap to another building?" The answer is simply "heck no." This is not necessarily because Superman and Spiderman are superheroes, but instead, because they believe in their distinct gifts, gifts that we all have within us just waiting to be activated. In other words, the emotional strength that F.I.S.T. equips you with, is about honoring the superpower of your true self. I don't know about you, but that is something I want to do every moment for the rest of my life.

TRUE SELF (P.U.M.A.)

1. **Power:** After you separate from what does not belong to, feel the power of your true self; your king or queen self. Furthermore, with "feeling" as your captain, access the yin and yang balance by "feeling powerfully," thereby commanding your ship.

2. **Unwavering belief:** Whatever is in front of you, regardless of what it is, know that, "I got this shit!"

3. **Mode of being:** Shine the light of your true self at all times and in all places because it is who you are.

4. **Act:** Bring things to completion to by taking action in order to make it a part of your being. Repeat the routine of F.I.S.T. not because it is a destination, but because it is a way of life and the very oxygen you breathe; which is being your greatest gift to humanity--YOU!

PART FOUR

PUTTING IT ALL TOGETHER

Now that you have worked through the process of becoming emotionally empowered, you will practice your emotional strength through the process of F.I.S.T. every morning, because it sets the foundation for the rest of the day. You will only need to fine tune specific parts of the process as it comes up during the day. Also, as you are engaging in the process in the morning, you will want to close your eyes the whole time, much like a meditation through which you can really feel it become a part of your being.

Below is a summary of the F.I.S.T. process. You will want to memorize all its steps (P.E.W.F. >> E.S.C. >> P.U.M.A.) in order to perform the whole process in a meditative state every morning upon rising with your heart and mind aligned as one.

113

UNLOCK YOUR EMOTIONAL POWER TOOLKIT

"Problems bring up feelings in us that existed before the problem ever happened."

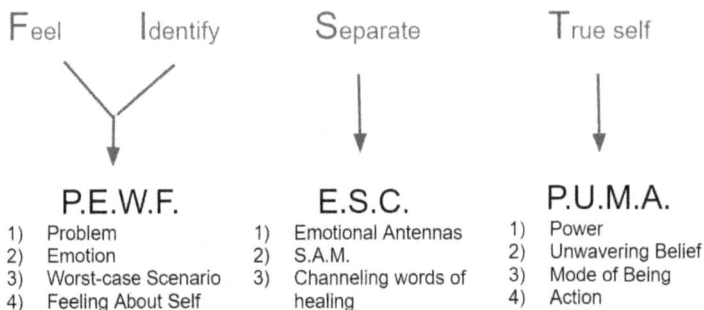

F_{eel}   I_{dentify}   S_{eparate}   T_{rue self}

P.E.W.F.
1) Problem
2) Emotion
3) Worst-case Scenario
4) Feeling About Self

E.S.C.
1) Emotional Antennas
2) S.A.M.
3) Channeling words of healing

P.U.M.A.
1) Power
2) Unwavering Belief
3) Mode of Being
4) Action

THE F.I.S.T. PROCESS CHEAT SHEET

Create the foundation for the rest of your day, by applying the whole F.I.S.T. process every morning. First, identify your feelings by applying the **P.E.W.F.** process by identifying the following:

1. **Problem** that brings up the strongest emotion in you: _____

2. **Emotion** the problem brings up: _____
   _____

3. Your **worst fear** (i.e. worst-case scenario) _____
   _____

4. The **feeling about the self** if your worst fear/ worst-case scenario were to come true. (Note: after

114

a few times you will automatically know how exactly this feeling comes from your_parents.):

_____

_____

_____

SEPARATE (E.S.C.), BY:

1. Feeling your core feelings with your **emotional antennas**,

2. Saying **S.A.M.** to the feelings you internalized from your parents through your emotional antennas, and then

3. **Channel S.A.Y.** by saying "Shit ain't mine and shit ain't yours either!" to your inner child, parents and generations before them because we were all emotional sponges who did not know how to use our gift of sensitivity.

4. Practice healthy boundaries of separation, by not only, saying a "loving no" to others who put their emotional stuff into your space, but also not putting your own emotional stuff in the space of others. In essence: let go of your responsibility for others so you can shine the light of your true self onto the world. Or in other words, "Shit ain't yours and you're the fucking shit!"

After you separate from what does not belong to you, you can feel the power of your -

True self with **P.U.M.A.**

1. Feel the **power** of your king and queen self, and take moments away from constant activity during each day, to command your ship by feeling powerfully.

2. Practice **unwavering belief** by telling yourself "I got this shit!" with whatever is front of you.

3. Express your true self as your **mode of being** by shining the light of your true self at all times and in all places.

4. Lastly, **act** in ways to honor your true self to make it a part of your being, which requires you to repeat the routine!

CHAPTER 16

❖

3 STEPS OF EMOTIONAL STRENGTH

THE PAIN
WE FEEL IS
THE PAIN OF
OUR INNER CHILD

HEAL
FROM THE GROUND UP

I am now going to streamline the F.I.S.T. process into three easy steps to which you can apply anytime your uncomfortable feelings or problems arise. Before you begin these three steps of emotional strength, I want you to first identify the place in your body where you feel your pain, or in other words,

117

where you physically store your feelings. Find any place between your heart space and your stomach area. After you identify where you store your feelings at, place one of your hands onto that area. Now, with your hand placed onto this "pain," I want you to recite the mantra, "the pain we feel is the pain of our inner child." I want you to reframe what pain is and no longer see it as your enemy, but rather, as the emotional wound of your inner child. Even as the feeling of emotional pain comes up in your life, I want you to embrace it on some level, because it is an opportunity to nurture and heal your inner child's pain who desperately needs your guidance.

DEEP ROOTED HEALING

The healing required to make you feel better and be the person you are meant to be is not a simple process where you can achieve a shift by simply changing the way you think. This healing is very similar to therapy, in the sense that it requires deep rooted healing. This means you have to focus on where it all began for you, which is your inner child.

The reason why it is important for you to guide your inner child throughout this process of emotional strength is because a child does not know how to use this gift of sensitivity, and let alone, even know that they have this gift. It can be very painful and traumatic as they feel the pain of their parents and automatically think it belongs to them. Imagine how painfully confusing it is for your inner child, the same child who is gifted with Spiderman-like sensitivity, trying to fix their parents' cries for help believing it is their own cry for help. I work with a lot of families and parents will bring their children to me eagerly hoping that I will help their child. What they come to realize, however, is that their child is only unknowingly and freely absorbing their parents' pain. It is time for you to guide and nurture your inner child because during your childhood, there was no one there to let that child know about this gift of sensitivity, how to use it and most importantly, that the pain they were feeling belonged to their parents.

Now that you have shifted the way you see your pain, from what was once your enemy, to an opportunity to acknowledge and nurture your inner child, you are ready to apply the three steps of emotional strength which you will find below:

3 STEPS OF EMOTIONAL STRENGTH ARE:

1. S.A.M.

2. Stay in my lane

3. I am the fucking shit

STEP 1: S.A.M. (SHIT AIN'T MINE)
(Children's version: Stuff ain't mine)

Anytime an uncomfortable emotion or problem comes up, it is your top priority to identify your feelings. Remember "problems bring up feelings in us that existed before the problem ever happened." As you are going through the P.E.W.F. process to uncover your feelings, you will find they will say something negative, but remember, these feelings are never true. You are just pulling the weeds of your feelings so that they don't overtake the yard of your true self.

If you don't identify these feelings, they will continue to control you. We constantly overthink and get lost in our thoughts, thus subconsciously enabling ourselves to avoid *feeling* our feelings. However, if you avoid your feelings, you cannot identify them, and your feelings will control you forever. The P.E.W.F. process allows you to bypass the endless overthinking and helps you identify your feelings so that you can separate yourself from them. As a refresher, P.E.W.F. stands for:

1. Problem

2. Emotion

3. Worst fear and worst-case scenario

4. Feeling about the self (if your worst fear came true)

Imagine how it would make you feel about who you are if your worst fear came true. One of the following two feelings (which cause almost all our pain) will come up:

1. Feeling of failure
2. Feeling of not existing

It is important to note that it is very common to carry both feelings of failure and of not existing within ourselves. For example, when I communicate with others, I fear that I will fail by saying something wrong and, as a result, causing the other person not to want to associate with me. If this were to come true, I would feel like I don't exist.

After you have identified your feeling as the feeling of failure and/or the feeling of not existing, you can apply the P.E.W.F. process to your parents, and you will realize why "shit ain't mine." You will discover that both you and your parents carry the same core feelings, as you unknowingly internalized them from your parent(s) or caretaker (i.e. grandparent) since you were a child through your gift of sensitivity (i.e. emotional antennas.)

My father, for example, is always working and needing to be efficient or productive. He can be hypercritical of others if they do not do things the "right way." My mother's worst fear is death (especially of her loved ones) which would not make her feel like she does not exist but also a failure because she failed to protect her loved ones. Ultimately, my deepest worries and fears are rooted in the failing of failure and not existing that were only internalized from my parents (in other words,: S.A.M).

IS S.A.M. TRUE?

It may be challenging to recognize that these feelings of failure or not existing do not belong to you. However, just as I mentioned in the very beginning of this book, I grew up as a child with a mother dealing with severe panic disorder. When my fiancée asked me to enact a sound to reflect the feeling of stress I was carrying, I started hyperventilating. My mother is always worried about health and safety because the thought of death brings up feelings of not existing. My grandma was outcasted by her father after he remarried because her stepmother did not want her father to associate with her. Even when Japan was invading China during WWII, her father was reluctant to protect her with her life on the line due to his new wife's demands.

This feeling of not existing then trickles down to me as I absorb it from my mother like an emotional sponge. For example, my fiancée struggles with being on time, and every time she is late, it makes me angry because her disregard for punctuality makes me feel that I do not exist. However, this feeling of not existing is just what I internalized as an emotional sponge from my mother since I was a child.

INNER CHILD S.A.M.

With your hand placed on the area in your body where you store your feelings at, use that physical touch to connect with your inner child and tell them:

"Shit ain't yours."

(Children's version: "Stuff ain't yours")

Basically, let your inner child know that their parents' feelings, that they unknowingly internalized as a child, simply do not belong to them.

THE OTHER SOURCE OF THESE FEELINGS

It is indeed true that the feelings of not existing and failure, are in part internalized from your parents. However, unlocking your highest potential for emotional empowerment and truly completing this process can only take place if you understand that these feelings also stem from another source (I will explore this in further detail as we uncover the next step).

STEP 2: STAY IN YOUR LANE

I want you to view this world as a global highway and know that everyone has their own sacred path in life, which is their sacred lane. Honoring it, is honoring your true self which is your greatest gift, to not only yourself, but to all others. Your sacred lane, which is your true self, is the very reason why you exist. With everyone in their own sacred lane and reason for existence on this global highway, there is something that disrupts this balance.

FEELING RESPONSIBLE FOR OTHERS

The reason why we steer into the lanes of others is because we feel responsible for them. Feeling responsible for others is what causes us to abandon our sacred lanes, and jump into the lanes of others while attempting to drive the vehicle of their life for them. Everybody has the freedom to choose any thought, action or feeling. Consequently, feeling responsible for others and going into their driver's seat is robbing them of this essential beauty and freedom of life. You are not helping others, but actually enabling them by being a crutch, if anything.

Additionally, even the common human desire to control is a symptom rooted in feeling responsible for others. Evidently, you can see that the natural tendency of control is to control what is out of our control, which is associated with that which does not belong to us.

"I'M A FAILURE"

When you feel responsible for others, you are essentially jumping into their lane and driving the vehicle of their life for them. Because it is impossible to drive the vehicle of life for another, you will inevitably feel like a failure.

The feeling of failure comes from feeling responsible for others. For example, I'm always fearful of disappointing others or making others angry, inconveniencing others, ultimately because I feel responsible for others. When I send a text or an email, I frequently worry about saying the "wrong" thing, potentially making others angry. To share another example, with my wedding coming up, my greatest fear is to not sleep well before the wedding day and, in turn, disappoint all of my dearest friends and family, including my fiancé, for not having enough energy to be present in the moment, one of the most precious moments of my life.

WE TRY TO SAVE IN OTHERS WHAT WE COULD NOT SAVE IN OUR PARENTS

I know I keep talking about not sleeping well, but interestingly my sleep problems only came about after meeting my fiancée. I am not blaming her as the only cause of my sleep problems, but what I do know, is that she triggered an underlying and hidden pain from my childhood because her pain is very similar to my mother's pain, which is an intense fear of not existing. The reason why my feelings of failure and not existing became intensified after meeting her was because I subconsciously saw her pain as an opportunity to save in her what I could not save in my mother.

It is almost as if I was reliving my childhood, because the same intense pain I felt in my mother, when I had to comfort her through her panic attacks as a child, was the same intense pain I felt around my fiancée. Of course, this is all happening subconsciously for me and I am not consciously aware of it. But knowing this now helps me to separate from my knee jerk responses to try to save her, or even to put up a wall against her behavior, only causing me to take on the pain. (I mentioned before how aggressive boundaries with others by putting up a wall against their behavior only makes us sponges to their pain.)

To give an example of what I mean, my fiancée has the bad habit of wanting to sleep very late by binging on the internet. I even resort to turning off the internet at a certain time to stop her from doing this. Some nights, she is adamant about using the internet late at night and the fear of her using the internet to no end keeps me awake, because I feel so responsible for her health and well-being.

I feel responsible for my fiancée and obsess about her bad choices. When my fiancée is in pain, I feel like I'm in pain. This kind of responsibility and extreme emotional entanglement serves no one and hurts me and my relationship.

"I DON'T EXIST"

The reason why we feel we do not exist, and do not matter, is because we abandon our sacred lane, which is our reason for existence.

For example, when I don't sleep well, I panic because me being decapitated of energy feels like death to me. If I die, I don't exist. Furthermore, if I get poor sleep, then I will have no energy the next day, making it impossible to be productive, thus making me feel like a failure.

Yet, the feeling of not existing and failure "caused" by poor sleep, is just me projecting these feelings onto the "problem" of poor sleep. I also fear that poor sleep will lead to me looking old and ugly, rendering me as unwanted by others, ultimately confirming my deepest fear all along, the fear that I do not exist.

For instance, although I'm excited about getting married very soon, I have to be honest that I am a bit hesitant about having a family. As much as I would love to have a family, I feel having children would lead to me having to sacrifice my life that much more. I realize now that I have already sacrificed my entire life in order to save others by making their pain into my pain.

VISUALIZE

When you feel feelings of failure, responsibility for others and even control, visualize yourself jumping into the lanes of others and getting into the driver seat of others while impossibly trying to drive the vehicle of life for another, inevitably making you feel like a failure and a failure to others. Just as when you feel like you don't exist, envision yourself abandoning your sacred lane, which is the reason for your existence, thus making you feel like you don't exist.

In order to stay in your lane, practice telling yourself to "surrender responsibility for others," and "surrender your responsibility for your parents." In doing so, you can finally see the magnitude of the harm you are causing to yourself, your inner child, and to others.

"When you feel responsible for others, you become an emotional sponge for all their pain."

Feeling responsible for others turns other people's pain into yours, which becomes your kryptonite, breaking you down physically, emotionally and mentally. It feels like a living nightmare because it feels completely hopeless, as if there is nothing you can do to fix the pain of others. This is especially true when you believe it belongs to you. Remind yourself that you are not an emotional sponge, but, a source of light. You have to separate and surrender responsibility from what does not belong to you to actually have the ability to help others.

Note: There is a difference between "duty" and "responsibility." For example, you have the duty as a parent to nurture, support and guide your child. However, you should not constantly feel responsible for your child, since this would mean jumping into their sacred lane (driver's seat) and trying to live their life for them.

INNER CHILD VERSION:

With your hand placed onto where you store your feelings at, tell your inner child to "stay in your lane" and more importantly "surrender your responsibility for your parents." The reason why you can feel so responsible for other and take on their pain so easily is because your inner child feels responsible for their parents, which is their world.

STEP 3: YOU ARE THE FUCKING SHIT
(Children's version: YOU ARE DA BOMB!)

After you separate from what does not belong to you and you stay in your lane, you can then feel the power of your true self, which is the reason for your existence, all of which reinforces that you are the fucking shit.

DEFINE YOUR TRUE SELF IN TWO SEPARATE WORDS

Define your true self in two separate words that describe the essence of your true self. Your true self is your source of power, love, joy, peace, wisdom and love. Your true self is why you exist.

As you are thinking of how to define your true self, remember it will not be words like "compassionate" "kind" or "caring" because helping others is not the means but the after effect of your true self.

YOUR TRUE SELF IS YOUR CONNECTION TO LOVE

Your true self is why you exist and is why you were created. Simply by feeling the beauty and power of your true self connects you with your divine creator, be it Love, God or the Universe (whichever creator you identify with) and therefore, your true self is your ultimate source of peace, power, wisdom, joy and love. Your true self is the beacon of light you shine onto the world.

YOUR TRUE SELF IS WHO YOU ARE, NOT WHAT YOU DO

After you define the essence of your true self, remember that your true self is not based on what you do. We are constantly thinking and doing because we falsely believe that the moment we stop our thoughts and actions, we will instantly cease to exist. Your greatest beauty and power come from who you are (just as you are!). Your self-worth is not dependent on anything you accomplish or don't accomplish. Realizing this has really changed my life. I used to always feel the need to be productive. I feared that making a mistake would lead to me failing, which would make me feel that I no longer exist because my existence depends on what I produce and on my "success." Don't fall into the trap of hunting for success and acknowledgment. Instead, turn your life into a masterful self-expression of the infinite beauty and power of your true self.

LOVE IS IN CONTROL

Constant thought and action are symptoms of seeking control. Ask yourself, do you frequently find yourself seeking control? We normally seek control for what is out of our control. Thus, control is a symptom of feeling responsible for others. When you find yourself seeking control, gently remind yourself to "surrender control" because "Love is in control." Or if you follow religion then tell yourself "God is in control." It helps to put your hand on the place of your body where your inner child resides and tell them, "Love/God is in control" so they can relinquish their false responsibility for others and their parents.

FEEL THE POWER OF YOUR INNER CHILD

I want you to place your hand on the same physical space where you once felt the "pain of your inner child," this time, feeling the power of your true self. Feel your mini true self there (i.e. "The peaceful explorer"), in your inner child, because you were created perfect, whole and powerful. With your hand placed onto them, tell them:

"You are the fucking shit."

Children's version: "You are da bomb!"

3-STEP INSTANT EMOTIONAL TOOLKIT

Anytime negative emotions or problems come up, I want you to apply this 3-step instant emotional toolkit.

Remember not to approach these steps only with your mind, but to really feel each step of this whole process. Tell yourself "feeling is healing," as it connects you to love. When you are ready place your hand where your store your feelings and where your inner child is, tell yourself the following:

1. **S.A.M. = Shit ain't mine**

   ➢ **Note:** have children say "Stuff ain't mine"

   ➢ **Apply the P.E.W.F.** process to yourself and your parents and you will see how you internalized your feelings from your parents since you were a child. A quick way to do this process is to immediately stretch a problem that is bothering you into your worst fear or worst-case scenario and think if it were to come true if it would bring up feelings of failure or not existing. After you have identified which feeling it is, you can see which of your parents you internalized it from.

   ➢ **Tell yourself "S.A.M."** while you breathe out these feelings that do not belong to you. This allows you to really feel all that does not belong to you leaving your body.

   ➢ **Inner child's version:** Tell your inner child, "Shit ain't yours." (Note: Children say "Stuff ain't yours.")

2. Stay in my lane

➢ View this world as a global highway and see how feeling responsible for others and even the desire to control causes you jump into lanes of others and try to do the impossible and take control of their driver's seat leaving you feeling like a failure. Furthermore, see how you abandon your sacred lane which is your reason for existence making you feel like you don't exist.

➢ Ultimately, staying in your lane means telling yourself to surrender your responsibility for others and your parents. Remember, if you do not surrender your responsibility for others, all of their pain will become your pain. When that happens their pain becomes your kryptonite that breaks you down physically, emotionally and mentally. Above all, it denies your true self, which is your greatest gift to yourself and to all others.

➢ **Inner child's version:** Tell your inner child to "surrender your responsibility for others and your parents." Tell them to "stay in your lane" and honor their reason for existence.

3. I am the fucking shit!

➢ **Note:** have children say, "I'm da bomb!"

➢ After you separate from what does not belong to you and stay in your lane, you can feel the power of your true self. Your true self is your source of power and love and more importantly, it is your reason for existence. Honoring your true self will make you feel like you are the fucking shit.

➢ Feel the power of your true self defined into two separate words.

➢ Remind yourself throughout the day to stop constantly thinking and doing (i.e. needing to be productive) as if your existence depended on it. Better yet, tell yourself to surrender constant thoughts and activities because they are a symptom of control. Feel the power of your true self: who you are – just as you are – is the reason why you exist.

➢ At the root of constant thoughts and actions is the desire to seek control. We typically seek control of what is out of our control. Therefore, control is a symptom of feeling responsible for others. Surrender control to allow love (your creator, be it God/the Universe) to be in control. With your hand on the place in your body where your inner child resides, tell them, "Love is in control" or "God is in control" so they can relinquish the painfully impossible responsibility they hold for their parents.

> Inner child's version: Tell your inner child "You are the fucking shit." (Children say, "You are da bomb!") Feel the power of the mini true self (defined by two separate words) within your inner child. Feel the beauty and power of your true self, which is your ultimate connection to your creator (i.e. Love, God, the Universe), for it is why you were created. Feel and imagine your true self as a beam of light shining onto the world and all throughout the Universe.

CHAPTER 17

❖

STAY IN YOUR TEMPLE

YIN AND YANG BALANCE OF YOUR MIND AND TEMPLE (YOUR BODY)

We live in our "headspace" by consuming ourselves with constant thought and action. Your mind is important, but it is only one half of the necessary yin and yang balance that needs to be grounded with the connection to your body, which I call your "Temple." Your mind becomes what you have come to know as the "ego" and there is a fine line from crossing into this territory and abandoning your Temple. Moreover, if you live exclusively in your headspace and are constantly thinking and doing, you are actually disconnecting from your Temple and its ability to feel.

Your Temple is your sacred source of power, peace, wisdom, joy and love because it is how you connect with your creator; whatever you want to call it - God, Love, the Universe, etc. You gain access to your Temple by feeling within it. Remember, "feeling is healing," as it connects you to your creator. However, consuming yourself by on living in the confines of your headspace, you automatically disconnect yourself from your source of peace, power, joy and love because you have disconnected from your creator.

I'm not asking you to disconnect yourself from your mind completely, but rather, to simply balance it and anchor it by staying in your Temple and feeling within it. Your thoughts are your ship, but without a captain, your ship has no direction whatsoever. Within this analogy, visualize your captain as the act of feeling within your Temple, for "feeling is healing," as it connects you to your creator.

THE ROOT OF ILLNESS IS NEGLECTING YOUR TEMPLE

I strongly believe the reason why we encounter physical problems with our bodies is because we neglect our Temples and do not connect with them by feeling within them. In fact, the large majority of my clients who have come to me seeking physical well-being have had unresolved emotional issues at the root of their physical problems. I'm not saying in any way that we do not need to take care of our bodies physically, but want to emphasize that it is even more important for us to simultaneously take care of our Temples in their entirety, acknowledging our Temples as our emotional and spiritual centers as well

Consequently, it is no surprise that physical ailments and conditions can often stem from our neglect to connecting with our sacred Temples by feeling within them.

WHY POSITIVE THINKING DOESN'T WORK

Positive thinking does not work, because the root of your thoughts and feelings are in your Temple. Negative feelings and thoughts lie in your Temple because your gift of sensitivity lies in your Temple. You misuse your gift of sensitivity when you feel the pain of others so much so that you believe their pain belongs to you and ultimately, is your responsibility. When you believe others are your responsibility, your Temple then becomes an emotional sponge for the pain of others.

The "Ego" attempts to project your feelings onto an external problem to give you the illusion of protecting you, but it removes you ever further away from the root of your feelings and thoughts which are being stored in your Temple. You can only truly remove the weeds of your feelings by uprooting them from their roots, not by simply removing them at the surface, which is the effect that positive thinking has. By going to the root of your feelings and thoughts, which lie in your Temple, you are able to truly separate yourself from them.

Now that you are practicing being more present with your Temple, you are ready to apply the P.E.W.F. process in a new, different, but equally transformative way.

GETTING TO THE ROOT OF YOUR FEELINGS THROUGH THEW P.E.W.F. PROCESS

You can easily find yourself infinitely lost in your endless thoughts, all-consuming emotions (i.e. anger, anxiety and depression) and seemingly hopeless problems. It is very important at this time to apply the P.E.W.F. process within your Temple. (P.E.W.F. = Problem / Emotion / Worst fear / Feeling about the Self)

If you use your headspace alone (the Ego) to apply the P.E.W.F. process, you may run into many barriers because the ego does not want you to feel. Identifying your emotion, worst fear and your feeling about the self (i.e. failure or not existing) are all things your ego wants you to desperately avoid because it deems them as too "painful." However, applying the P.E.W.F. process by feeling and experiencing the whole process within your Temple immediately connects you to your creator, which is your sacred source of peace, wisdom, power, joy and love. This makes connecting with your feelings no longer painful but tremendously healing, because your Temple is your sacred connection to your creator. Thus, when you connect with your feelings by feeling them within your Temple you give these emotional wounds the medicine of love from your creator it needs to begin to mend and be washed away.

Example:

For example, this very chapter you are reading is something I had to add after thinking I had already finished my book with the previous chapter. As I'm writing this chapter I constantly feel like a failure because I feel like my book will never be done. Interestingly, when I connect with my Temple by feeling within it, instead of reverting back to emotionally numbing myself with busyness and busy thoughts, I realize for the first time on why I get so frustrated with my fiancée being so late all the time. Her frequently being late "prevents" me from doing the things I *need to* get done or else will make me feel behind or in other words like a failure.

As you can see, the extent to which my fiancée's tendency to be late angers me is simply me projecting my feelings of failure onto an external problem. No matter what, I am able to settle with my fiancée about her issues with punctuality, it will do nothing to tend to and heal the feeling of failure I feel within my Temple.

As you get to the part of the P.E.W.F. process where you identify your "Feeling about the Self," you know there are two of the most common feelings which are the feelings of failure and not existing. Both of these feelings are internalized from your parents, through your emotional antennas, since you were a child. The question is, how do you use your Temple, to separate from these feelings that do not belong to you?

141

ACTIVATE YOUR TEMPLE

In order to truly separate yourself from these feelings that do not belong to you, you want to activate your Temple. You activate your Temple by staying in your Temple and very importantly feeling within it. As you remember, "feeling is healing," since the act of feeling makes you one with your creator. As you are connected with your Temple, everything that does not belong to you, simply dissolves and washes away.

On the other hand, when you live solely in your headspace by overthinking, you abandon your Temple which is your tool and gift for sensitivity. When you misuse and neglect your tool for sensitivity, your Temple becomes an emotional sponge and storage space for the pain of others. By staying in your Temple and feeling within it, you will have activated your Temple and everything that does not belong to you will naturally dissolve and wash away.

EMOTIONALLY NUMBING YOURSELF THROUGH BUSYNESS

You may feel the urge to numb yourself emotionally by, for example, constantly using the internet, immersing yourself in social media, overworking, overthinking or overeating. Numbing yourself emotionally is both tempting and deceiving at the same time, because it seemingly is a "release" and an escape from your emotional pain and discomfort. However, remember, emotional pain is a wound and if you avoid it by numbing it or escaping it by projecting it onto an external problem, the wound will only grow and eventually consume you; very much acting like a cancer.

Constantly remind yourself to feel within your Temple because "feeling is healing." As you can see, your Temple is sacred because it is your ultimate connection with your creator, and thus your Temple is consequently your source of peace, power, joy, wisdom and love. Staying within your Temple and feeling within it, automatically dissolves and washes away all the negative feelings and emotions that does not belong to your true self.

THE TWO SOURCES OF THE FEELINGS OF FAILURE AND NOT EXISTING

The feelings of failure and not existing come from two sources, with the second source being more prominent. The first source, as discussed earlier, is internalized from our parents, since we were children through our emotional antennas (i.e. S.A.M. = Shit Ain't Mine). We unknowingly misuse our gift of sensitivity as children by feeling the pain of others, namely our parents, so much so that we absorb it and falsely believe it belongs to us.

The second and more prominent source of our feelings of failure and not existing belongs to our feeling of responsibility for others. Feeling responsible for others is how you misuse your gift of sensitivity by feeling the pain of others so strongly that you not only feel that it belongs to you, but ultimately, is your responsibility. Your Temple, which is your sacred physical body and source of your spiritual and emotional self, is your gift of sensitivity. When you feel responsible for others, though, your Temple becomes an emotional sponge for their pain. However, because you cannot fix what does not belong to your Temple, you will inevitably feel like a failure. Furthermore, feeling responsible for others is what makes you abandon your sacred Temple, which is your reason for existence, in order to invade the Temples of others, causing you to feel like you do not exist.

THE IRRESISTIBLE FEELING OF RESPONSIBILITY FOR OTHERS

Although feeling responsible for others can greatly pain you, at the same time, it feels almost impossible to let go of. For example, my strong feeling of responsibility for my fiancée can bring up immense anger and feeling of being hopelessly out of control. She is constantly using the internet and consuming sugar as a way to avoid her feelings and it feels like her actions eat away at my core and soul. There are often times where no matter what I say, or do, she will not listen. I almost can't stop thinking about it, even though I am privately doing my own thing.

When I catch myself feeling so immensely and painfully responsible for my fiancée, I continually remind myself that I have abandoned my sacred Temple, while at the same time, invading her sacred Temple as well.

Note: There is a difference between duty and responsibility. I have the duty as a future husband to take care of my wife and to love her. But, I can never hold myself responsible for her because that would be invading her Temple and intruding on her sacred lane.

Staying In Your Temple Is How You Most Powerfully Help Others

Your Temple is your source of light, peace, power, wisdom and love because your Temple is your ultimate connection with your creator. Therefore, when you stay in your Temple by feeling within it, it turns you into a source of light onto the Universe. This is how you become greatest gift to others, and help others in the most powerful way possible. Contrarily, feeling responsible for others and abandoning your Temple, while invading the Temple of others is how you help no one and only hurt yourself.

Surrender Control To Allow Love to Be In Control

You can often find yourself seeking control in order to resolve your problems. It is important to also know that every time you seek control, you are abandoning your sacred Temple and invading the temples of others, while playing the role of your creator who is the only true entity in control.

Seeking control, which is the power of your creator, blocks the love of your creator from flowing through you. When you stay in your Temple, by feeling within it, you naturally surrender control to allow your creator to be in control and to flow through you like a beam of light.

By staying in your Temple, while simultaneously surrendering control, your Temple then becomes a source of light because your creator is then able to flow through your Temple and outwardly to the Universe. Staying in your Temple, while surrendering control, immediately releases the pain of blocking the love of your creator from flowing through you.

Take a moment right now to surrender all control. Feel every morsel of control released from your Temple. Surrender control to allow love to be in control. This how you stay in your Temple, which is your connection to your creator, and thus your ultimate connection to your source of peace, power, joy, wisdom and love.

SEPARATING FROM FAILURE AND NOT EXISTING AT ITS ROOT

By staying in your Temple, you automatically separate from the feeling of not existing and failure. The root of your feelings of not existing and failure come from abandoning your sacred Temple and trying to impossibly fix what belongs to the sacred Temples of others. When you stay in your Temple by feeling within it, you no longer feel like a failure for not being able to impossibly fix what does not belong to you. You also no longer feel like you do not exist because you are staying in your Temple, which is your reason for existence.

STAYING IN YOUR TEMPLE IS A WAY OF LIFE

Make the habit of staying in your Temple and feeling within it a constant meditative way of life. Do it every morning, upon waking. Do it before you go to bed. Do it instead of numbing yourself emotionally by becoming a slave to your smartphone. It is easily seen from observing society, just how addicted we are to our smartphones, which reflects our addiction to numbing ourselves with constant thought and action.

It is critical for all of us to continually ground and anchor ourselves by staying in and feeling within our Temple because it activates our sacred Temple, which is our ultimate connection to our creator and washes away all the pain that comes from abandoning our Temple in the first place.

BE GENTLE WITH YOURSELF EVERY TIME YOU FALL

When you catch yourself feeling yet again like a failure or not existing, or feeling consumed with anger, depression and anxiety, or lastly, feeling responsible for others; ultimately you want to be gentle with yourself. The reason why is because your pain is a deep-rooted pain and trauma that stems from your inner child and childhood. This pain you are dealing with, is the same one you are internalizing and feeling responsible for; it is the pain of others since your childhood, which I believe is the greatest and most prevalent pain of humanity.

I have had clients who have been sexually abused by their parents and yet, when I applied the P.E.W.F. process to them and their parents, their greatest pain did not come from the sexual abuse, but rather, the pain they internalized from their parents as their own and thus felt responsible for. I have seen countless children, as clients, who are brought in by their parents. These parents' sole focus is usually to only help their child but the child is only unknowingly and freely absorbing and internalizing the pain of their parents as their own. A child is too young to know how to use their gift of sensitivity the right way and their parents did not know how to guide them on how to use this gift because they themselves have yet to understand the unresolved issues of their own inner child. With this newfound understanding, this is a time to guide your inner child in a way they weren't able to be guided.

Just as you would patiently and lovingly guide a child who is falling while learning how to ride a bike, patiently and lovingly tell yourself to brush off the dirt every time you fall, you can consistently remain in your Temple by feeling within it and thus honoring it.

As you are trying to understand and practice the process of emotional healing and empowerment, remember this "place" of healing and empowerment is not a destination. Do not think, "when will I get there?" because once you stay in your Temple by feeling within it, you are "there." All your pain will have washed away by staying in your Temple and you will automatically feel whole, complete, powerful and one with your creator.

CHAPTER 18

❖

THE STORY OF TFS (THE FUCKING SHIT)

The origination of this book's title, "You are the Fucking Shit," has a personal story behind it which is both funny and transformative. Read on to hear this personal story of mine which led to creation of this book!

When I was in coaching school, our class did an interactive group exercise where we had to act out our "captain," our inner guide. My classmate asked me what I wanted to do to embody my captain and I told her that I felt like standing on a chair and emphatically banging my chest like athletes do after making a great play. I told her I felt shy, but she encouraged me to do it. So I went up to a chair, stood on it and started banging my chest. My classmate asked me again what else I wanted to do to embody my captain. At this time, still standing on the chair, I bended over to whisper to my classmate, "I kind of want to yell out 'I'm the fucking shit' but there is absolutely no way I'm going to yell that in class." My classmate told me to go ahead and do it and she was just amazing in making me feel so safe and secure as I was breaking the limits of my comfort zone. I took a deep breath and yelled at the top of my lungs, "I'M THE FUCKING SHIT!" My teacher chuckled and told the class with a hint of a smile, "Okay, I think we are done with this exercise."

A couple of hours later, we did another exercise in pairs where we talked about our life purpose. After the exercise, we reconvened in a large circle. One of my classmates confessed to the group how she did not know her life's purpose, and it was really bothering her. Another classmate walked up to her and started coaching her. He helped her identify her life purpose and asked her to state it proudly to the whole class while standing on her chair. My classmate felt it had been so helpful for her that she asked the entire class to take turns stating their life purpose to the class while standing on her chair. Each of my classmates took turns doing that. Most of my classmates said very peaceful, eloquent statements, such as "I'm the lighthouse that illuminates the world" or "I'm a safe ocean that provides transformation for others." Finally, it was my turn. I got on the chair, looked at my classmates, spread both arms, took a deep breath and yelled "I'M THE FUCKING SHIT!" Everyone in the room exploded with laughter. After that class, my classmates would refer to me as TFS, short for "The Fucking Shit." This experience is something my classmates and I always remember when we meet. Initially, I was known as the quiet person in my class, but the more comfortable I became with myself, the more my classmates were able to see not only my calm intuitive self but also my playful goofy self. It is when you honor your true self that you truly have your greatest, most valuable impact on others.

TFS is obviously not just me. We are all TFS! After you separate from what does not belong to you, by staying in your lane and staying in your Temple, you will feel the power of your true self, which is your reason for existence. Your true self and your Temple are what connects you to your creator and thus are your source of light, power, peace, wisdom, joy and love.

Your life purpose is to be your true self, because it is the source of light you shine onto the world. Do not deny the gift of your true self and jump into others' lanes and invade others' Temples by living out their pain – as if their pain was your responsibility. Shit ain't yours! Stay in your lane, stay in your Temple and live out your true self because you are and always will be… the fucking shit!

HEAL THE WORLD FROM WITHIN

Writing this book became possible only after I found my own emotional strength, which entailed having to repeatedly dig deep within myself and to search for tools to heal my emotional pain and trauma. Yes, it is true that living with this emotional pain made me feel like I was often living my worst nightmare. However, through my day-to-day trials and tribulations, and through writing this book, I was able to find the answers I was looking for and piece together the missing pieces which brought about the healing and empowerment of my own soul.

I am sure if you are reading this book, you probably have a strong desire to help others. You may feel that your "emotional problems" are getting in the way of you being there for others, but remember that the gift of healing you give to yourself is the very same gift of healing you will give and are meant to give to all others. Everything I have shared with you in this book comes from my continual healing and empowerment. Take the opportunity to make your emotional difficulties and pain into the gift of healing you give to both yourself and to all others. As you share with others, you will heal yourself. As you heal yourself, you will in turn be able to share this same healing with others. These two halves of cyclic healing feed off each other and it is an essential part of what it means to be a part of humanity.

To give you a personal example, it took me awhile to publish this book, although I had seemingly already completed, because I kept on trying to "perfect" it. During this long standstill of seeking perfection, I received a client who told me he had a problem of never finishing anything he set out himself to do. At his current job, he recently told himself, he would fully commit himself to doing good work and giving it his all. Despite his determination, he still ends up giving lackluster effort and doing just the bare minimum to get by.

I asked him, was it because he was afraid that if he were to give it his all, and he were to still fail, then that would ultimately confirm that he is a failure. My client confirmed this was true for him, and it was in that moment, that I could see my own reflection. I was holding back on publishing my book, by trying to endlessly find ways to "perfect" the book. I later, shared my feelings with my fiancée, and she told me, "You are polishing a diamond for the world to see. However, this book is not your diamond. You are the diamond. The book, and your future books, will be the process in which you polish the diamond that you are for the world to receive." This powerful statement hit me at my core and finally gave me the final push to finish my book, while seeing its true purpose as a means and not an end.

Ultimately, I hope that the messages and principles echoed throughout this book empower you to polish both the diamond and The Fucking Shit that you are, advocating for your own healing, which is the same gift of healing you are meant to share with all others.

What's Next?

Spread The Word To Empower Others

The purpose of this book is to provide humanity the first critical step of emotional healing and empowerment, so we can begin to heal the world from within, together. Share this book's message with everyone. Have fun with it, e.g. take a picture of yourself with the book and share it on social media, including the hashtag #YOUARETHEFUCKINGSHIT.

Please Share An Honest Review On Amazon

The more reviews this book has, the more it will allow others can know of this book's message on emotional healing and empowerment, which will help it spread globally across humanity. To leave a review, search this book's title, "You are the fucking shit," on Amazon (available on all global Amazon sites) and scroll down the page until you see the button to leave a review.

PRIVATE SESSIONS

If you need further assistance so you can honor your truest self, which is your greatest gift to humanity, I provide private sessions via video calls (Skype or Face-Time) or phone calls and work with individuals, relationships, families and children. For more information about my services, please visit www.healfromthegroundup.com/services

I can also be reached via email at michael@healfromthegroundup.com

SPEAKING ENGAGEMENTS AND MEDIA INTERVIEWS

If you would like to request me as a speaker as well as for interviews and workshops (including in-person, phone and online/via video), please contact me at: michael@healfromthegroundup.com

STAY CONNECTED

Go to my website www.healfromthegroundup.com and sign-up for my newsletter and you will receive a FREE powerful video presentation I created for my book so you can actively understand how to apply its emotional healing methods to your life. You will also receive the newest updates about events, articles and new books by Michael Hsu and Heal From the Ground Up.

Follow Michael and Heal From the Ground Up on social media to join a community of people healing from the ground up together!

FACEBOOK GROUP:

www.healfromthegroundup.com/community

FACEBOOK PAGE:

www.facebook.com/healfromthegroundup

INSTAGRAM:

www.instagram.com/michael4humanity

VISIT MY WEBSITE FOR MORE INFORMATION:

www.healfromthegroundup.com

❖ ABOUT THE AUTHOR

All my life I really enjoyed learning about how to better one's emotional well-being, but growing up, there was never an ounce of me that believed I could help others in this regard. In fact, I would always ask friends for personal advice, so much so that one friend even told me to stop bugging her, and to just trust myself. Therein came a turning point for my life, which was led by the end of a relationship. The breakup forced me to understand what was going on mentally and emotionally with my ex, in a way that even surprised me. The revelations I made gave me the confidence that I could guide others with their emotional well-being.

At that time, I had already established my practice, in which I would help others, with their physical well-being, as a holistic health practitioner. With the confidence in my seemingly newfound ability, I began working with clients, who came to me for their physical well-being, and started asking questions about their emotional well-being. What seemed like a sudden downpour of tears came from the overwhelming majority of my clients. This gift that I had uncovered for healing and empowering others emotionally came so naturally to me, that there were times I felt guided, as I was guiding others. So assured that I wanted to pursue this as part of my life's purpose, I sought to further my education by completing coaching school, to develop and fine tune my natural ability.

In my practice, helping others is a spiritually transformative experience for me, because everything I share with my clients, is what I had to first learn for myself. In fact, every time I see a new client, I see them as a mirror into what I still need to reaffirm in my own life.

In 2010, I started my private practice called Heal from the Ground Up, which targets the root of emotional, mental, and physical well-being so we can see life-lasting and transformative changes. As a professional life coach, holistic health practitioner, global love activist and now author, I facilitate people in the process of unlocking their emotional strength, heal their body from the ground up and shine their light onto the world. As such, everything I share with you in this book comes from my own healing and transformation, which began with cultivating my emotional strength. Ultimately, this gift that healed and empowered me emotionally, is the very gift I share with you in this book.